Crochet Liberation Front

First Ever Book!

Edited by

Laurie "Camanomade" Wheeler

Crochet Liberation Front ™ First Ever Book

Book Design: Laurie Wheeler

Cover Art: Kristin Kesecker

First Edition Laurie Wheeler

2008

Laurie Wheeler

Camano Island, WA

98282

Camanomade@earthlink.net

Breach of copyright means our member will hunt you down like the dog you are...

CLF Manifesto

By Laurie Wheeler
Founder, High Head Poohbah, Fearless Leader
& Global Dominatrix of the CLF
©2007

We are the Crochet Liberation Front!
We are both male and female, all races, creeds, and nationalities.
We hook and we are proud.
With our hooks we make lace, household items,
Dresses and sweaters, socks and slippers,
Tablecloths and bedspreads,
We make jewelry and sculptured art.
We are limited only by our creativity and imagination.
That which we make *is* beautiful.
We refuse to be pigeon-holed into any single category.
We refuse to accept the myth that we are less than other arts and crafts.
We will not apologize for our love of all that is hookable.
We refuse to continue in the need to have other crafts to make us valid.
We are valid in and of our own nature.
We refuse to accept the stereotypes that keep us downtrodden and unsupported.

We are the Crochet Liberation Front and WE hold our hooks high!

Dedication

(yeah, it's long...but worth the read)

This book is dedicated to the fine men and women who comprise the Crochet Liberation Front.

Without your participation this book, and our group would not exist.

There are too many people (over 2100 strong!) to start naming names for all their support!

To my moderators, thank you for holding down the fort in my book provoked absence.

Special thanks goes to our group on Ravelry.com, the message board has been a sanctuary for me personally, during a difficult year.

Big thanks to Danielle (aka Laracroft) without her this book would never have happened...(Beware her suggestions).

Special thanks go out to Myra Wood for her quiet whispers behind the scenes and her encouragement to go for it, thank you beautiful lady!

Extra special thanks go out to Casey and Jess, (and Bob too) for putting up with our crazy brand of crochet on Ravelry.

Without Ravelry none of this would have EVER happened.

Thank you.

And yes, like a mother hen, I am proud of all of you.

Grand thanks to my husband, Jeff and to my children Sara and Yousif for putting up with me and my crazy ways.

Tu Blathe is always worth living for...

To Ann M. Hopkins for opening my world and showing me that I really was the artist I always wanted to be: I'm a real girl now, thank you!

To Bec, her big feet that first got me published and those damn sexy goats...

Finally to Nancy Wilson who was my newspaper advisor/teacher at Gladstone H.S., Gladstone, Or from 1983-1987. Everything I know about layout, I learned from you (And with computers we don't have to worry about my not having depth perception with the lines anymore!)

Acknowledgements

To all those who tested patterns and for some reason or another go unmentioned.

Thanks to David, the head librarian at Camano Island Library, for his words of encouragement and flipping the switch on the wi-fi router, so that I could download email without tears of frustration due to my ugly dialup situation at home. To the Island County WSU Beach Watchers for putting up with me hiding in their office at Cama Beach .while I worked on the book...To the folks at Elger Bay Grocery Store (Camano Island, WA) for keeping the coffee brewed and hot!

To Guillem , Mr. "Laracroft" for the great tutorial photos.

Pyo, who not only contributed gorgeous patterns, but helped test patterns.

Margarita Catellerio for her work on the Ave Maria Tree Skirt (she made all 140 motifs!)

Julie (SkyDramini) for her work making up the Peek A Book Play Time Negligee.

Heather Riggs, my cousin, for pouring over the book with me and holding my hand.

Sara Wheeler who will one day forgive her mom for using photos of her in the book and will hopefully, one day see how gorgeous she really is! And to Yousif for reading out one of the patterns so I could transcribe it to the computer. You did really well buddy, and I wasn't joking about it being an important job!

Bec Thomas for taking phone calls at midnight to check out a variety of things on the web for me so I didn't have to deal with dial up, and for chasing the pigs back in the pen...that was a day I don't want to repeat! Thank you!.

Alison, aka Smurf, for putting up with my less than silent screams in Ravelry private messages, when the book would not behave.

Kristin Kesecker for her brilliant graphic arts abilities and making a really kick ass book cover, and holding my hand through the technical things, you really are a Techno-Goddesss.

To all the snobby pointy stick players who insulted my work directly or indirectly, there would be no CLF without you, thanks for the opportunity. (Not that you're reading this anyway, cause why would a pointy stick snob buy the book?)Finally ,huge acknowledgements to our people in the CLF for remembering that we are a PRO-Crochet group, and not an anti-knitting group. For all the words of encouragement, you guys have no idea what good timing you have!

Contributors & Co-Conspirators in this great tome of crochet goodness…

Part I ~ Set My Picot Free

- ❖ USA   Candi Oldfield (Candicmt)   ~ CLF Coffee Cozie
- ❖ USA   Alia Smith (Crocheteer) ~ "The Five Mistakes",
- ❖ USA   Julia Meek Chambers (Bikermom)~ Flaming Hook Tapestry Crochet Pattern
- ❖ USA   Tracie Barrett (TracieCrochets)~ "Everyman Wants a Hooker"
- ❖ USA   Sharon Falkner(Share32006) ~CLF Patch
- ❖ USA   Elisa Cleveland (Summergirl) ~ Raise Your Hooks Fingerless Gloves
- ❖ France Annette Petavy (AnnettePetavy) ~ " My Road to Free Form"
- ❖ UK   Kate Torode (Kaet) ~ Natcromo Free Form CAL
- ❖ USA   Adrienne Via (Grieney) ~ Golly's Broomsticks
- ❖ USA   Tracie Neil (MsCrochets) ~ "The Makings of a Crochet Group"
- ❖ USA   Jennifer Reeve (Craftkitten) ~ Crochet Dragon Scale Socks
- ❖ Ireland Orla Breslin (Stitchlily) ~ "Irish Revolution-A life time of crochet"
- ❖ USA   Mary Zeman (Marykz) ~ Granite To Go
- ❖ USA   Karla McCalmont (karlaamm) ~ Very Versatile Vertical Stripe Beanie
- ❖ USA   Amiee Woolwine (Aimeecrochets) ~ " My New Hooks"
- ❖ France Pyo (Pyogazel) ~ Scarlett Blossom

Part II ~ Hookalicious

- ❖ USA   Jennifer Reeve (Craftkitten) ~ Crochet Cabled Fingerless Gloves
- ❖ USA   Carol Ventura (Tapestrycrochet) ~ Prelude to Tapestry Crochet UFO Bag
- ❖ USA   Carol Ventura (Tapestrycrochet) ~ Tapestry Crochet UFO Bag
- ❖ USA   Shevon Retske (Fibernerd) ~ "You Got Math in My Crochet" (Or on the grid)
- ❖ France Pyo (Pyogazel) ~ Ondine
- ❖ UK   Shirley MacDonald (Cherryred) ~ Sticks and Strings and Other Things
- ❖ Uk   Zuleika Lambe (Crochetzu) ~ Cabled Slouch
- ❖ France Julia Vaconsin (jujustrickt) ~ Phoenix Mitts

Introduction

A message from the Big Cheese, High Head Poohbah, and Fearless Leader of the CLF:

This book came about because of discussions about publishers and their bias against crochet as a saleable media. We went from whining, to someone saying "Hey the CLF should have a book!" So, in the Judy Garland and Mickey Rooney tradition "Hey gang, let's put on a show!", this book was conceived. When I agreed to put it together I had no idea what it would look like, or what kind of patterns would come in (or if any would come in!). I knew I could put a good book together, but I had never done this large of a collaborative work before... This book is indeed an amateur work, amateur meaning that someone does something for the love of it. Even professional designers can be amateurs if they do it out of the love of the craft. That very premise is what this book is about, because that is the Crochet Liberation Front's mission. We are here to liberate crochet and those who wield the hooks from the oppression of an industry that has tarred us with an ugly brush.

We have one thing to say to them: "In your face Industry Monkeys!
Read this book and WEEP!"

On a serious note it is important to remember that this book is a unique collaborative endeavor. It is by and for the Crochet Liberation Front members and was formatted to show the diversity, depth and breadth of not only our talents but who we are as people. I chose not to change the language to standardize grammar and syntax, our contributors are from around the world: Australia, France, Philippines, Ireland, Scotland, England, Spain, and the United States are all well represented in these pages. Remember that people spell differently depending on which English they use, and I think standardization has caused a real loss of variety, individuality and character in many realms of life, not just crochet. I changed nothing in the make-up of the patterns, I (as editor) merely formatted them into the package that you are now holding. We have worked hard to ensure there are no errors, but things do indeed occur, we'll have a website for errata and will have it listed on Ravelry.

To you the crocheter, this book presents you with the opportunity to walk with us, the CLF, on this journey. After all, we are people first, people who crochet. In these pages you will find more than patterns, because we know that those patterns become offerings of love. How so? Do you not make gifts for others, loved ones and strangers, even if you only make things for yourself, is that not showing yourself love? We know that holding hook in hand is a way to get through the ups and downs of life, and we know that most likely you crochet alone. As you join us in this book, you will never have to be alone again, now you have us. We are the CLF; we are here to liberate the hook and the hands, minds and hearts that they wield.

Sincerely your servant in this cause,

Laurie Wheeler (Camanomade)

The Illustrious History
of the Crochet Liberation Front

By Laurie Wheeler

With the combination of frustration and fatigue, on a hot July morning I founded the Crochet Liberation Front.

I did not expect anyone to join. I invited no one, and I had no graphics for a banner. I just threw it out there, and went on my way. No one was more shocked when I saw two people had joined. We ranted about the way we who hook are treated in yarn stores, and by snobby pointy stick players. We growled about the lack of crochet samples in stores, lack of availability of hooks, books, patterns and more. We asked questions, and demanded answers. To be honest, I didn't start the group out to be a real organization, its conception was just a sarcastic joke.

Why a joke? Ok, an angry joke? Because I tried to voice my feelings in other online crochet venues only to be hushed, shut down, and politely shut up. No one wanted to be political. I didn't think that commenting on the poor wages designers, contract crocheters, and the hands that make all the crocheted items you find in stores was all that political, or I should say radical. I mean, we all crochet here; shouldn't we want to do better? Should not we want to make more money for what we do? To me that is just common sense. When I formed the CLF I didn't think I would have any takers, and that my friends, is why I say it was a joke.

But truly the joke was on me. I wasn't the only one out there who felt as deeply and passionately about our creative expression with hooks and yarn. Am I glad you joined! I reveled in each "inflammatory" post, each call for equity and parity in the craft yarn consumer market.

When someone called for a banner to be made, and voila one of the members was a graphics artist, I was amazed... Anarchy hooks were born! Did you notice that the top two hooks make a little heart? I love that best of all in the graphic!

.

It wasn't until late September, 2007 when I went to the CGOA event in Oakland, armed with hooks, crocheted lovelies, and the infamous CLF T-shirt, that I decided to make the CLF more than just a joke. The reception to the idea was glorious. It made people laugh, not at us, but with us. There was an acknowledgement even by the pointy stick players that indeed, we who hook are often hard done by.

As the fall of 2007 progressed, our membership exploded, we weathered a few minor growing pains, and we began to call out the publishers of books, and magazines asking for answers to such burning questions as:

 * Why aren't there more complex patterns available?
 * Why don't the more exclusive yarn companies advertise to us?

The answers were often less than desirable. As much as we, the membership of the CLF called out that we are not cheap, or lesser than our pointy stick playing cousins, we were told in round about ways that indeed that is how we are viewed. Really? Cheap? No one has seen my stash, or yours I bet.

Sometime during the approaching winter holiday season, Danielle (aka Laracroft) suggested we start our own book. I didn't pause long for thought; I did beg to have until after the New Year to get organized. And I went to work on the plotting, and the scheming. What you hold in your hand is the product of that scheming, and much plotting.

I put out the call for submissions, and they started to trickle in. I was totally amazed at the quality, and quantity of submissions. Sure there was some hand holding involved, sure some people were scared to submit for publication for the first time. Yet, you did submit, and as you flip through the pages of this book, you will see that we, who hook, are awe inspiring.

We have more work to do, more hooks to raise, more good deeds to accomplish, and more projects to finish…but the CLF is here to stay. You, my friend, are part of that illustrious history, and you should feel proud about your participation in this amazing group of people!

Laurie Wheeler (Camanomade)
Fearless Leader, Big Cheese, Global Dominatrix of the CLF

ix

Hook on, Hook long my minions!

What the Heck is the Crochet Liberation Front?

Who? Committed Crocheters from across the globe! With over 2,000 members; we are all colors, faiths, genders, life styles, urban and rural.

What does the CLF Do? Promote crochet and those who crochet. We do this in the following ways:
1. Awarding members and others for outstanding crocheted goodness on our blog
2. Writing to companies and asking for policies to change (such as advertising directly to us! Or making simple changes such as writing "crochet and knit" versus what you normally see.)
3. Spread the word about shops (Local Yarn Stores) who are friendly towards our craft or better yet help promote it, via our Crochet Friendly LYS List. This list is completely member driven and no one pays to be on the list. (This list can be found on our Ravelry group page)
4. Spread the word about crochet related books, websites, real life activities and more.
5. Contact companies large and small requesting minor (sometimes major) changes to include crochet in a way that is optimum for consumer and business...*(some people call it whining, we call it action...)*

How do I join? Right now we ask that you go to Ravelry.com* (if you aren't there already), and join our group there. Or you can visit our website and blog for a chuckle and send Laurie an email. Visit us at www.crochetliberationfront.com.

How do we get in the "Loop"? Once again, I urge you to join Ravelry.com and join our group on the message boards, but you can stay informed by listening to our podcast (CLF Global Domination Report) check it out at clf.mypodcast.com, our blog, web-site and if you get to trade shows look for folks wearing the CLF Buttons, we may even have a booth!

Why do we need the CLF? Maybe you do, maybe you don't. Membership is free and people are welcome to come and go as they please. We exist because we feel strongly that the yarn and craft publishing industry have been prejudiced against our beloved craft and we want that to change. We also wish to promote crochet to the world at large as something that is fun, creative, and an easy way to gain skills and confidence!

I'm a knitter can I join? Absolutely! We're not anti-knitting, we are Pro-crochet! We're not here to do the diplomatic efforts of bridging the crafts, we are here to promote what we enjoy. You can enjoy lots of crafts and still be in the CLF. We do not condone putting down knitters and discourage that treatment of anyone for any reason. We believe that all crafts are wonderful in and of their own selves. However, our craft has been maligned for quite a long time and it is our goal to dispel the myths and negative stereo-types that plague us.

A few more words...about Crochet and it's "Scene".

Crochet has been much maligned over the past few years in the needle work press. Even when publications seem to attempt at making nice to we who wield hooks, it's done in some kind of awkward "we love you anyway" kind of fashion.

As a life-long crocheter, I really have had enough of this nonsense. At first it was a mere annoyance, after meeting this bias up close and personal at various fiber art events, and even on crochet message boards I began to feel angry and eventually I just stopped buying books and magazines. Some of the most popular crochet tomes to date are ones that don't hold a great deal of interest for me personally. It appears to me that these books are intended to convert people over to the crochet cause, as I do not need converting, I prefer to have patterns that are chart orientated, and a little more on the complex side or perhaps I should say I'm tired of single crocheted scarf patterns done in different kinds of novelty yarns (duh, we can figure that out for ourselves).

I don't know that I'm ok with converting anyone to anything. Not that I want to keep crochet cloistered and inbred, oh quite to the contrary. I just believe that there has always been good crochet out there. If publishers and yarn companies would stop buying into the myth that crocheters are cheap and uncultured and allow their designers the free reign to create fashionable, wearable, and functional crocheted garments, toys, household décor, and accessories they may discover that there are more than a handful of willing consumers. What crocheters need are not more words in their patterns but measurements, schematics, and general construction information. We create fabric differently than our stick wielding cousins, not better, nor worse, just in a different manner. That difference should be celebrated not condemned or ignored, the sooner the yarn industry (which is the driving force of pattern writing) comes to this understanding the better things will be for everyone concerned.

I think we're hard to market to because so many of us haven't bought patterns, because they didn't learn to read patterns. They were taught basic stitches and told "bless you my child" and went on to discover what could be crocheted. Now, this is not every crocheters experience (especially those who have learned to crochet in the past five years), but I have heard this concluded from many of the minions in the CLF. In the past decade more of us have begun to read and use patterns, because more interesting patterns have become available. I learned to read patterns five years ago when I decided I wanted to create a better sock pattern, but I still prefer designing out of my own head than using someone else's ideas. What I hankered after was construction information, how to shape, how to make flattering lines, how to exploit my materials.

Lately, we've seen this information coming our way, and for that we say thank you to those who have listened. What can be done to further the cause? Get the yarn companies attention! I do not believe in bad yarn, I believe that all yarn has a purpose. Do you really want to make a cashmere dog blanket? If you do, you have a very lucky dog. As for me, I love my lab but not that much! Yarn companies need to understand that we do buy their yarn, but we'd like to see more than granny squares sewn together into skirts, jackets, and handbags (we know how to do that thank you very much), we want to see other projects, more complex stitches, or things that are easy but look complex!

Stop telling us we're cheap, unsophisticated, and from the wrong side of the tracks! Stop patronizing us with articles about how we can be more like our pointy stick cousins and gain acceptance. Stop spreading malicious rumors about what can and can't be crocheted. We who wield hooks are talented, creative, people who buy yarn and hooks when we feel the desire, for projects we may or may not get to. We are so varied in what we make that you'll find those who only use thread, and those who make toys, those who only do garments, and people who love to make pictorial afghans of the last supper. Some of us free form, and others use patterns, we have learned as children and as adults, some of us are teenagers and some are grandmothers, (gasp) some of us are male! Well, heck, go back and read the manifesto which sums up these thoughts more eloquently.

How to reach crocheters? Advertise to us first and foremost; show us beautiful and creative ideas for your products! Reach out to us! Yarn stores help sponsor a crochet guild in your area, offer more than just a basic "how to" crochet class. Offer something that is a bit more interesting, holiday themes, ornaments or gifts are often popular crocheted items.

To crocheters I say, STOP HIDING and APOLOGISING! You are the creator s of wonderful things, and the holder of a crafting tradition that deserves accolades not derision! Stand up for your chosen medium, and make more wonderful things, crochet in public, and stop trying to get the "snobby stick players"[1] to accept you. Cool kids don't go around trying to get other people to like them, they know they are cool and other people feel it.

I will leave you with the wise advice a dear friend gave me years ago, "Don't get mad, get organized!"

It is time for those who wield the hook to come away from their solitary creating, join together in solidarity and proclaim our rightful place in the world of needle arts. If we do not do so, we will continue to lose magazines, hook suppliers, yarns, and patterns. Together we can show people just how fabulous crochet can be!

This book is just a beginning…more is to come. We shall cause crochet to dominate the world!

---

[1] Snobby Stick Players only refers to the snobs who use pointy sticks who put down crochet. Many stick players are not snobby in the least and we love them dearly!

Part I

Set My Picot Free

> **All humans are bound by chains of some kind: doubt, fear, pain, worry....**
>
> **In crochet we have found a way to make chains that shall set us free....**

"Set My Picot Free" was a phrase that came into being early on in the CLF experience. What does it mean?

There is no exact definition of the phrase, but it can mean...

"Back off you mean minded pointy stick player..."

"Finding the crochet hook size I'm actually looking for would be nice..."

"More than three colors of crochet thread would be more than a novel experience, it could border on a spiritual event."

"Being treated like a real person, with real money in an LYS would be really super."

"Having patterns with real substance, or articles that are relative and useful would make me actually buy a publication."

"Treat we who hook with respect..."

"Understand that for some of us, crochet is part of our heritage, or holds a special place in our hearts."

What does Set My Picot Free mean to you? If you haven't thought about it, read through this section. I, the Big Cheese, High Head Poohbah, and Fearless Leader of the CLF, promise you , the hand that wields the hook, that you shall be inspired.

Set My Picot Free is also an award! To drool over examples of award winning crochet yummy goodness, check out the Crochet Liberation Front Blog.
http://www.crochetliberationfront.blogspot.com

The Crochet Liberation Front Minions pulled out all the stops in their submissions...I hope you are as impressed as I was in making selections... Hooks Raised, CLF Salute!

Materials

Any worsted weight yarn in the following colors:

Black (MC)

Red (CC)

White*

Gold*

Hook: F (3.0 mm)

Sewing needle/Yarn Needle

Button

* Only small amounts of this yarn used.
Crochet Stitches Used:
(US Definitions)
Ch: Chain
SC: Single Crochet
Sl St: Slip Stitch

Comminque from Fearless Leader:
Candi won the CLF design competition on our message board on Ravelry!
Congratulations Candi & thank you for designing such a
great coffee cup cozy! Yummers!
Fearless Leader's coffee addiction thanks you!

CLF COFFEE COZIE

By Candi Oldfield (aka Candicmt)

© 2008 Candi Oldfeld Reproduced with Permission.

Body of Cozie: With CC (red)	
Base:	Ch 2
Rnd 1	SC 8 into second chain from hook, sl st into first stitch to join, forms first rnd. Ch1
Rnd 2	SC 2 into each stitch, slip stitch into first stitch, ch 1 (16 stitches)
Rnd 3	SC into first stitch , SC 2 into next stitch, repeat sc,sc 2, across rnd, join with sl st, ch 1 (24 stitches)
Rnd 4	As per round 2 (32 stitches)
Rnd 5	3 SC into first stitch, 2 sc into next stitch, repeat 8 times. Change to MC (black) for last SC, sl st to join, ch 1. (40 stitches)
Rnd 6	With MC(black) SC into each stitch, sl st to join. Ch 1 (40 stitches)

With MC	
Rnd 7	Sc into back loop (bl) of each stitch, sl st to join, ch 1 (40 stitches)
Rnd 8-9	Sc into each stitch, sl st to join, ch 1 (40 stitches)
You will now begin working in rows	
Row 1	SC into first 38 stitches, ch 1 turn (38 stitches)
Row 2	As per Row 1 (38stitches)
Row 3	**Making button flap:** SC into each stitch for 38 stitches, ch 15, ch 1 turn (38 stitches+15 ch)
R ow 4	SC into each stitch, ch 1 turn (52 stitches)
Row 5-6	SC into each stitch, ch 1 turn (52 stitches)
Row 7	To make button hole: SC into 47 stitches, ch 3, skip next three stitches, SC into last 2 stitches, ch 1, turn (52 stitches)
Row 8-10	Sc into each stitch, ch 1 turn (52 stitches)
Row 11	Sc into each stitch, do not turn, sc over edge evenly, join into first stitch of row 11.
Medallion (To be sewn on to the front of Cozy)	
Base	Ch 2
Rnd 1	Sc 8 into second chain from hook, join with sl st to first stitch of round.
Rnd 2	Ch 1, sc 2 into each stitch, sl st to join, ch 1 (16 stitches)
Rnd 3	(SC into first stitch, SC 2 into next stitch,) repeat 8 times. Sl st to join, ch 1 (24 stitches)
Rnd 4	(Ch 1, SC into next stitch, Ch 2, skip 1) repeat until end of round, join with sl st. bind off, leaving 6 inch tail for finishing.
Finishing	

With yarn needle sew medallion to front of cozy. Place cozy onto coffee mug to determine button placement, sew on button. Using yarn needle, and small amounts of yarn,embroider CLF and hooks to front medallion working through to the back of the cozy. Secure thread, weave in ends. (Note: make sure to put cozy onto mug BEFORE filling mug with hot liquid!)

"The Five Mistakes"

By Alia Smith (aka Crotcheteer)

In the brief time since I have taken up a crochet hook, I have often thought that one of the lesser reasons that I like crochet so much is that it's an underdog. Crochet is the yarn-world's red headed stepchild to the heir apparent… Knitting.

Yes, I secretly enjoy the fact that sometimes I need to defend my chosen craft to those who either do not know (or do know and chose to ignore) the value of crocheting as viable yarn-consuming option.

Nowhere is this battle more apparent than at a Local Yarn Store or, LYS.

I find that there are five easy ways that a LYSO (or Local Yarn Store Owner) can raise the ire of a crocheting patron and all but ensure that he or she …and his or her wallet…will never return.

#1 – Carry few, if any, crochet hooks. Make sure they are all the same size, the same brand, and are stored in such a way as to make it utterly apparent that knitting needles are the yarn-boss of them and they must be relegated to one small, milk-quart size section of what is a large and varied selection of twin pointy sticks. Never mind dusting them, as one day they will be discovered by the curator of an industry museum and the layers of grime in variegated shades of gray and brown will only add to the value.

#2 – Outdated Materials. Be sure that your books, magazines and patterns for crochet only represent 1-5% of your entire educational inventory and that they are at least three years old. Everyone knows that crochet is really only good for making granny square afghans and doll clothes and carrying anything more current and fashionable is just encouraging the illness and preventing them from learning to knit.

#3 – Yarniscm (or…we don't swatch your kind around here.) Make sure none of your lovely yarns are used in a crochet swatch or – WORSE! – an actual project. Seeing them will only give a crocheter more ideas and who wants someone buying up your entire inventory, especially when crocheters tend to use more yarn and use it up faster. Yarn will fly off the shelves left and right! The horror!

#4 – Smile condescendingly or make Crochetist jokes. Do it in such a way as to make us feel as though we are the yarn version of Julia Roberts to your Rodeo Drive haute couture boutique. We love that.

#5. "Don't know much about HDC…" Pleading ignorance and then doing nothing about it is one of the biggest mistakes an LYS can make. Hire someone who crochets part-time, barter time-for-yarn if you have to.

Better yet, when a customer mentions crochet, take notice. Ask them to teach a Learn to Crochet series at your location or ask them how you as an LYSO can improve your stock. One of the best experiences I ever had was when an LYSO sat raptly watching me swatch some Noro because she'd never seen it crocheted before.

To crocheters, a CFLYS (Crochet-Friendly Local Yarn Store) is the Holy Grail and when we find such a place, we shout your name, location, website and phone numbers from the rooftops. We give major points for even small efforts to make us feel welcome.

Crocheters may not all be sane, but we use a heck of a lot of yarn and we're as loyal as can be when we find an LYS who supports us. Isn't that the kind of customer you need?

Flaming Crochet Hook Pattern Notes and Directions by Julia Meek
Chamber (aka Bikermom) © 2008

Skill Level: Intermediate to advanced crochet skills. Requires prior experience with tapestry crochet technique, plus experience in working with fur type yarns-not otherwise as the stitch difficulty is relatively easy.

Suggestion: Count stitches carefully, because fur type micro-fibers are not forgiving, if you need to frog (rip out stitches). The fuzzy fibers like to tangle, if you do need to frog, do so in the following manner: go very slowly, pulling each stitch separately from the top loop first, ensuring all the "fuzz" is gathered before with each loop before moving to next stitch.

Materials

Yarn:

6, 50gr (93 yd) balls Moda Dea "Dream" in Black

1, 50gr (93 yd) ball Moda Dea "Dream" in Brown

1 similar ball of yarn in bright orange

Scraps of Red Yarn for letters "CLF"

(Optional: Various scraps of yellow and orange for shading)

Hook: Size I

Optional: Material for lining bag. It is highly suggested to do so by the designer.

Early on in the CLF Experience the Flaming Hook of Justice was born...thanks to Ravelry gad about town, Bubbo...

This flaming hook so inspired Julia (Bikermom) that she created this fun graph and chart...so all of us may wield the hook in solidarity! ~ Fearless Leader...

Main Body:

The chart is exactly the width and length of one side of the bag. **46 x 63 stitches**. Make the chart according to the key in single crochet, being sure to carry yarn colors as needed. Then make another panel to the same dimensions in black, or whatever other color you desire, 46 x 63 stitches. If you choose a different color for the back of your bag, it takes about 3.5 balls of the yarn above for the back side and strap alone. Crochet pieces together at bottom and sides.

Optional: Crochet a gusset to join the two sides to, depending on how wide you'd like *your bag to be.*

Designer notes:

I'm a freeform crochet artist and rarely use patterns myself. Hence this pattern is written from a free-formist's point of view. This pattern can easily be used with a variety of scraps for the back-side and strap, however you choose to make it. Mainly, you want to measure well and crochet to fit those dimensions.

This pattern can be enlarged easily by increasing the diameter of both yarns and hook. Just remember: as you increase your yarn thickness, all the colors must remain around the same thickness for your stitches and dimensions to come out right. If you cannot find the right color in a thicker yarn, you need to use multiple strands to create the effect of a thicker yarn. You can also consider plying your own.

Strap Options:

1. Single crochet a strap at least 1 inch wide and as long as you prefer your bag strap to be.
   Attach to sides of bag.

2. Use a strip of leather or belt webbing, cut to the length you prefer, and single crochet around it, top and bottom. Attach to bag. (This will add strength and stability to your strap.)

3. Use a heavy duty metal ring (found in the hardware section of large DIY Stores), or recycle a thick soda or water bottle ring. Crochet around it and then build upon that to create strap and attach to bag.

Key to the Flaming Crochet Hook chart:

🐟 - Black squares = the color of the Hook (I used brown)

▌ - Gray squares = the color of the letters "CLF"

🏵 - The color of the flames. (I used an orangey red *shorter* fur type yarn – Not Fun Fur)

🔵 - Optional shading for the crook of the hook (I used a darker brown). Make same color as hook if you decide against the shading.

x – Optional yellow highlighting. Make same as color of the flames if you decide against yellow highlights.

Optional special stitches:

/ - Denotes where a half stitch should be used of a certain color. I.e. "/." would denote half the stitch on the bottom should be of the flame color. "./" would likewise indicate half the stitch at the top should be of the flame color. If you choose not to use this half stitch, just use a full stitch of either color on either side of / to your choice.

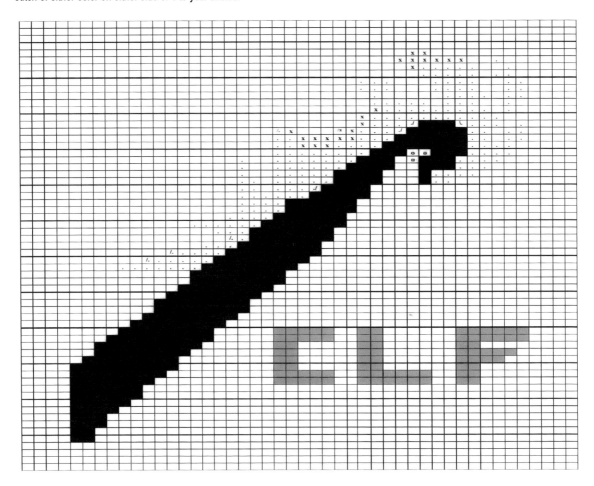

Every Man Wants a Hooker

(How Crochet Helped Me Meet the Man of my Dreams)

In early 2003 two things happened in my life. I got divorced and I picked up crocheting in full force. Were the two related? Yes. Crocheting kept me sane and gave me something safer to do with my hands (as opposed to strangling people). It became a semi-serious joke with my coworkers: If they didn't see me crocheting, then either something was blowing up at work or they needed to clear the building as I was about to end up on the six o'clock news.

I started dating someone and thought that it would work out. We had been best friends before dating and were already roommates (handy that). He knew about the crocheting and the yarn that was in the apartment. I figured he understood: Love me, love my yarn. Well, long story short, he didn't. He complained when I crocheted while we watched TV. He complained when I crocheted in the car on long trips. He didn't understand that I could multi task and talk and crochet at the same time. A year and a half later, we broke up.

I waited a year, throwing myself into my yarn (sometimes literally) and learning more about myself. I got to the point that I felt I could date and not feel the need to jump into a relationship. So I put up a profile on Match.com. I was honest in my profile. I don't remember exactly what I wrote now, but I know it said something along the lines of, **"I crochet. I crochet a lot. I will crochet while we watch TV, I'll crochet in the car on long trips, and sometimes I crochet while waiting. I have a lot of yarn. I have a yarn addiction and I'm not looking for help. If any of this bothers you, then don't bother."**

I went on a few dates. Guys thought I was funny, and thought I was exaggerating in my posting. Until they realized that I attended a crochet group twice a month, crocheted sometimes at work (when the boss wasn't looking), crocheted in waiting rooms and in my car while waiting to meet up with people. Most of the guys made somewhat disparaging remarks about a gal my age doing what they considered "granny work". They either never got a first date (or a response) and none of them got a second date.

One day I got an email from a guy named John. He started out by telling me that his grandmother crocheted and one summer tried to teach him. Uh huh. I'd heard that line before. I emailed him back, we corresponded a bit, and he seemed nice. He asked me why I crochet, what had gotten me into it. I told him about how I use it as a stress reliever. How crochet is very meditative to me. How I love being able to take a "piece of string and a bent stick" and make really cool things. He commented how he should probably learn since he had a high stressed job. Sure. Okay. Heard that one before, too.

A couple of weeks into our correspondence my mom had to have surgery. I was stressed and told everyone I would be out of touch for a bit. One afternoon I got online and John was on the instant messenger program we used. He sent two messages that ended up winning me over. The first: "How is your mom doing?" (he remembered!). The second: "Are you doing okay? Are you crocheting to help with the stress?" Yeah, that won him his first date.

I'll spare you the details of the first couple of dates (yes, he was the only guy to get a second date). We talked about all kinds of things and he never balked at my crocheting. On our third or fourth date he met a few members of my crochet group at a party. He showed a great interest in the scarf I was showing them (yes, we take crochet to parties). They all liked him and suggested that he come to our next meeting. Now, he thought this was very nice. I knew it was his "second interview" with them. We told him we didn't expect him to crochet. We just wanted him to sit with us and hang out.

Imagine my surprise when he showed up and walked in carrying a skein of Bernat Baby Coordinates in blue and a hook. He bought the yarn and hook by himself because he wanted to make a blanket for his friend who just had a baby. We were the first two to show up to the meeting and he sat there with me, in the middle of a crowded bookstore cafe, and had me show him how to start. He'd already done a few chains because he remembered how to do that. His chains were good, but I thought I'd show him how to do a granny square instead. It was easy and would grow to the size he needed pretty quickly. The first meeting he sat there, dealing with the looks from other guys in the cafe, working very hard on his blanket. By the end of the meeting, those same guys were nodding. John was the only guy sitting in the middle of a group of about fifteen women. He was the center of attention as he worked every double crochet. It was cute, he'd concentrate so hard on the crocheting that he couldn't participate in the conversations. He was floored as to how we could chat and crochet at the same time, sometimes not even looking at what we were doing.

Fast forward a year later. John and I are now living together and planning our future. I have my own yarn studio in our home. He goes to every crochet meeting with me, and is able to chat and crochet at the same time. He takes me to yarn shops. He picks up the crochet magazines when he sees them. He's completed not only the baby blanket, but also contributed a square for our friend's comfort-ghan, and is now making a blanket for his cousin's baby. He gets upset when I go to a yarn shop, not because I went and bought yarn, but because I've gone without him.

I, now work from home as a crochet instructor and designer, *something I could never have done without his support.* He brags on me to everyone, showing my blog with pride to family and coworkers. We often have conversations about how a garment is put together and how it could translate into crochet. He is beginning to understand the different fibers and their uses. There is often yarn all over the house, and he doesn't mind. I made him a hook holder for Christmas and he loved it.

I cry a little inside whenever I hear women talking about how they have to hide their yarn purchases from their significant others. I know I'm lucky and a rare breed. But, I think if we were to all teach our significant others how to crochet, there would be less hiding of the yarn stashes. John respects what I do as an artist, and is my biggest cheerleader. He is also now a proud member of the Crochet Liberation Front.
So to all the singles out there, my advice is this. Do not hide what you do. State upfront that you are a crocheter and expect it to be respected just like any other hobby or passion. You may not find a winner right away, but it's a great way to weed out the duds.

And you never know, you may find a crocheter of your own.

Materials:

Steel Hook Size 8 (1.5mm)
Steel Hook Size 12 (1.0mm)
DMC Embroidery Floss:
    4 skeins White
           (Blanc) –
           wound
           on/into 4
           bobbins/
           balls.
    1 skein Black
(#310) – divided on/into 2
bobbins/balls.
    1 skein Red (#321) -
divided on/into 2
bobbins/balls.
    1 skein Lt. Old Gold
(#676)
Sewing needle

Gauge: Main Patch is 10 sc /
in (2.5 cm) on size 8 hook

Terms:

ch = chain	sc = single crochet
dc = double crochet	sl st = slip stitch
hdc = half double crochet	yo = yarn over

CLF Patch

By Sharon Falkner (Share32006) © 2008

Not everyone's husband will let them attach a patch to their leather bomber jacket, so here are some other ways to use your patch. You could put some iron-on interfacing on the back and sew it to a jacket, beret, jeans, backpack (to proudly show your CLF Pride while hiking across Europe), or black canvas tote to use as your favorite new crochet project bag. Basically, anything you could attach any other patch to! Have fun!

I wanted this to be something every member of the CLF could make, so we could equally show that we hold our hooks high. If you can single crochet, you can do this!

Note: This pattern uses American crochet terminology.

Finished Size: Approximately 2 ½ in x 3 ½ in (6.5 cm x 9 cm)

Note from the Big Cheese:

This pattern is written with a lot of detail. I could have changed that to make it shorter. But, I think it is a great tutorial on how to do color work with multiple bobbins. So, if you've wanted to try something more ambitious, this pattern is a great first step to doing some of the more complex color work/tapestry crochet pieces in the book!

Tips:

Working thread: It's sometimes confusing with all the bobbins to know which thread is the working thread and which is the carrying thread. I found that by placing a piece of clear tape with a mark of some kind on it (i.e. a simple pen mark) on the bobbin of the working thread, it was easier to keep track of it.

Starting a carrying thread: I start my carrying thread when the first single crochet is almost complete (just before the last yarn over). Place the thread to carry over the working thread, then yarn over and finish stitch. Be careful not to pull on the carrying thread so it doesn't come out.

Color changes: Color changes are done before completing the stitch. Start the single crochet stitch as usual but before the last yarn over, switch to the new color, yarn over and pull through the two loops on the hook of the previous color. Then continue in new color as stated in the instructions.
On even numbered rows, the threads are held on the front side of the fabric. For these rows, before changing color, pull the threads to the back side of the fabric, then continue color change. This will keep the front very neat and allow for fewer threads to weave in at the end.

Tangles: I found two things helpful to deal with tangles. First, keeping the bobbins wound short when not in use helped to prevent a lot of tangles. Second, stopping every couple of rows to untangle what mess there was helped keep the tangles to a minimum as well.

Crocheted Crochet Hooks: This is really tiny work that may be easier using a magnifying lamp.

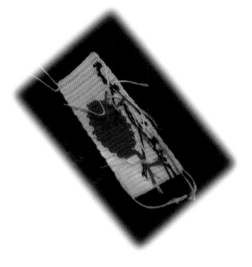

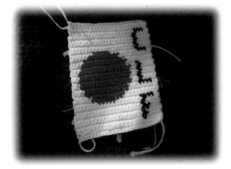

Body of Patch

Base chain	With a size 8 (1.50 mm) hook and white thread, ch 26.
Row 1	sc in 2nd ch from hook, while starting a white carrying thread (see tip on starting a carrying thread). Continue carrying this thread and sc in each base chain across. Ch 1, turn. (25 sc)
Row 2	Bring carrying thread up from the side and over to the side opposite you (front side of fabric). Place hook in first sc of previous row, with the carrying thread to the right of the hook. With working thread, yo and pull the carrying thread to the left over the working thread. Yo again with working thread and pull through to complete 1 sc. Pull carrying thread slightly to minimize the "bump" on the edge. *(Use this technique on all edges for the remainder of the pattern)*. Continue carrying the white thread and sc in each sc across. Ch 1, turn. (25 sc)
Row 3	Following the technique above for the edges, sc 5, switching to black in the last stitch (see tip on color changes). Continue with the white carrying thread until row 9 (see row 9 for details). With the new black working thread, sc 1, switching to the white working thread. Drop the black thread. With the white working thread, sc 19. Ch 1, turn. (25 sc)
Row 4	Sc 19, switching to black in the last stitch. With black, sc 1, switching to the white working thread. Drop the black thread. With white, sc 5. Ch 1, turn. (25 sc)
Row 5	Sc 5, switching to black in the last stitch. With black, sc 1, switching to the white working thread. Drop the black thread. With white, sc 19. Ch 1, turn. (25 sc)
Row 6	Sc 19, switching to black in the last stitch. With black, sc 2, switching, in the last stitch, to the white working thread. Drop the black thread. With white, sc 4. Ch 1, turn. (25 sc)
Row 7	Sc 5, switching to black in the last stitch. With black, sc 1, switching to the white working thread. Drop the black thread. With white, sc 19. Ch 1, turn. (25 sc)
Row 8	Sc 19, switching to black in the last stitch. With black, sc 1, switching to the white working thread. Drop the black thread. With white, sc 5. Ch 1, turn. (25 sc)
Row 9	Sc 2, switching, in the last stitch, to black from the previous row. (Note: This will pull the black thread over several stitches on the backside of the fabric, but will allow for fewer ends to weave in.) With black, sc 4, switching, in the last stitch, to the white working thread (which will again pull the thread over several stitches on the backside o the fabric). Drop the black thread. With white, sc 7, switching to a new red working thread in the last stitch. Drop both white threads. Use the new red working thread, and starting a new red carrying thread (see tips on starting a carrying thread), sc 5, switching to a new white working thread in the last stitch. Drop both red threads. Use the new white working thread, and starting a new white carrying thread (see tips on starting a carrying thread), sc 7. Ch 1, turn. (25 sc)
Row 10	Sc 5, switching to the red working thread in the last stitch. Drop both white threads. With red, and red carrying thread, sc 9, switching to the white working thread from the previous row in the last stitch. Drop both red threads. With white, and white carrying thread, sc 11. Ch 1, turn. Break off black thread from previous row. (25 sc) (You should now have 4 white bobbins and 2 red bobbins attached to your work.)

Row 11	Sc 10, switching to the red working thread in the last stitch. Drop both white threads. With red, and red carrying thread, sc 11, switching to the white working thread from the previous row in the last stitch. Drop both red threads. With white, and white carrying thread, sc 4. Ch 1, turn. (25 sc)
Row 12	Sc 3, switching to the red working thread in the last stitch. Drop both white threads. With red, and red carrying thread, sc 13, switching to the white working thread from the previous row in the last stitch. Drop both red threads. With white, and white carrying thread, sc 9. Ch 1, turn. (25 sc)
Row 13	Sc 2, switching, in the last stitch, to a new black thread. Drop the white working thread and continue with the white carrying thread. With black, sc 4, switching, in the last stitch, to the white working thread. (Note: This will pull the white thread over several stitches on the backside of the fabric, but will allow for fewer ends to weave in.) Drop the black thread. With white, sc 3, switching to the red working thread in the last stitch. Drop both white threads. With red, and red carrying thread, sc 13, switching to the white working thread from the previous row in the last stitch. Drop both red threads. With white, and white carrying thread, sc 3. Ch 1, turn. (25 sc) (You should now have 4 white bobbins, 2 red bobbins, and 1 black bobbin attached to your work.)
Row 14	Sc 2, switching to the red working thread in the last stitch. Drop both white threads. With red, and red carrying thread, sc 15, switching to the white working thread from the previous row in the last stitch. Drop both red threads. With white, and white carrying thread, sc 2, switching to black in the last stitch. Drop the white working thread and continue with the white carrying thread. With black, sc 1, switching to the white working thread. Drop the black thread. With white, sc 5. Ch 1, turn. (25 sc)
Row 15	Sc 5, switching to black in the last stitch. Drop the white working thread and continue with the white carrying thread. With black, sc 1, switching to white working thread. Drop the black thread. With white, sc 2, switching to the red working thread in the last stitch. Drop both white threads. With red, and red carrying thread, sc 15, switching to the white working thread from the previous row in the last stitch. Drop both red threads. With white, and white carrying thread, sc 2. Ch 1, turn. (25 sc)
Row 16-17	Repeat rows 14-15
Row 18	Sc 2, switching to the red working thread in the last stitch. Drop both white threads. With red, and red carrying thread, sc 15, switching to the white working thread from the previous row in the last stitch. Drop both red threads. With white, and white carrying thread, sc 2, switching to black in the last stitch. Drop the white working thread and continue with the white carrying thread. With black, sc 1, switching to the white working thread. Drop the black thread. With white, sc 5. Ch 1, turn. (25 sc)
Row 20	Sc 3, switching to the red working thread in the last stitch. Drop both white threads. With red, and red carrying thread, sc 13, switching to the white working thread from the previous row in the last stitch. Drop both red threads. With white, and white carrying thread, sc 9. Break off black thread from previous row. Ch 1, turn. (25 sc) (You should again have 4 white

	bobbins and 2 red bobbins attached to your work.)
Row 21	Sc 10, switching to the red working thread in the last stitch. Drop both white threads. With red, and red carrying thread, sc 11, switching to the white working thread from the previous row in the last stitch. Drop both red threads. With white, and white carrying thread, sc 4. Ch 1, turn. (25 sc)
Row 22	Sc 5, switching to the red working thread in the last stitch. Drop both white threads. With red, and red carrying thread, sc 9, switching to the white working thread from the previous row in the last stitch. Drop both red threads. With white, and white carrying thread, sc 11. Ch 1, turn. (25 sc)
Row 23	Sc 2, switching, in the last stitch, to a new black working thread. Drop the white working thread and continue with the white carrying thread. With black, sc 3, switching to white working thread in the last stitch. (Note: This will pull the white thread over several stitches on the backside of the fabric, but will allow for fewer ends to weave in.) Drop the black thread. With white, sc 8, switching to the red working thread in the last stitch. Drop both white threads. With red, and red carrying thread, sc 5, switching to the white working thread from the previous row in the last stitch. Drop both red threads. With white, and white carrying thread, sc 7. Ch 1, turn. (25 sc) (You should again have 4 white bobbins, 2 red bobbins, and 1 black bobbin attached to your work.)
Row 24	Sc 19, switching to black in the last stitch. Drop the white working thread and continue with the white carrying thread. With black, sc 1, switching to the white working thread. Drop the black thread. With white, sc 5. Break off the red threads and any unused white threads from the previous row. Ch 1, turn. (25 sc) (You should now have 2 white bobbins and 1 black bobbin attached to your work.)
Row 25	Sc 5, switching to black in the last stitch. Drop the white working thread and continue with the white carrying thread. With black, sc 1 switching to the white working thread in the last stitch. Drop the black thread. With white, sc 19. Ch 1, turn. (25 sc)
Row 26	Sc 19, switching to black in the last stitch. Drop the white working thread and continue with the white carrying thread. With black, sc 1 switching to the white working thread in the last stitch. Drop the black thread. With white, sc 5. Ch 1, turn. (25 sc)
Row 27-28	Repeat rows 25 and 26
Row 29	Sc 2, switching, in the last stitch, to black. (Note: This will pull the black thread over several stitches on the backside of the fabric, but will allow for fewer ends to weave in.) Drop the white working thread and continue with the white carrying thread. With black, sc 3, switching, in the last stitch, to the white working thread. Drop the black thread. With white, sc 20. Ch 1, turn. (25 sc)
Row 30	Sc 25 across. Break off black thread from previous row. Ch 1, turn. (25 sc)
Row 31	Sc 25 across. Finish off. Weave in ends. (Note: all ends should be on the backside of the fabric.) (25 sc)

Notice from the Big Cheese:

All the patterns in this book utilizing the CLF, Crochet Liberation Front initials and logos have been used with the permission of CMHS Yarn & Designs.

Finishing:

Cut a piece of red floss 18 in (46 cm) long. Pull out 2 strands from this piece. Using the 2 strands together, embroider the strings of the ball of yarn:

Use 1 strand of remaining cut gold floss to sew the crocheted crochet hooks onto patch forming an A. (Note: One of the long hooks and the short hook will actually need to be turned upside down for this step.)

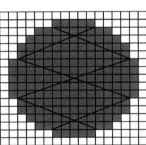

Long Hook (make 2):

Base Chain: With a size 12 hook and 1 two strand piece of gold floss, ch 47.

Row 1: Hdc in 3rd chain from hook. Hdc to 7 from end of base chain. (38 hdc) Sc 3, sl st 3, sc 1. Ch 3 turn.

Row 2: Dc 1. Finish off. Weave in ends.

Short Hook:

Base Chain: With a size 12 hook and 1 two strand piece of gold floss, ch 28.

Row 1: Hdc in 3rd chain from hook. Hdc to 7 from end of base chain. (21 hdc) Sc 3, sl st 3, sc 1. Ch 3 turn.

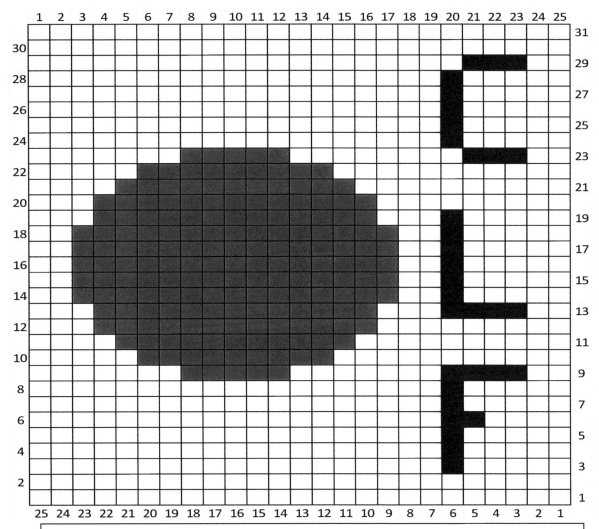

If your patch so far isn't exactly rectangular, pull it into shape before continuing with border.

Using Black, join with slip stitch in any corner. Ch 1. While starting a black carrying thread (see tip on starting a carrying thread). Sc 3 in same space and in each corner. Continue carrying this thread, and sc around patch. You should have 25 sc across the top and bottom and 30 sc along the sides. Finish off. Weave in ends.

Block lightly to straighten/even out edges and train the patch to lie flat.

Raise Your Hooks ~CLF Fingerless Gloves

Designer Notes on Technique:

<u>Foundation Double Crochet (fdc)</u>-Chain 3(counts as first stitch), yo, insert hook in third chain from hook, yo, pull through (3 loops on hook), yo, pull through <u>1 loop only</u> to form base chain (3 loops still on hook). Next yo and pull through 2 loops twice to make dc. *YO, insert hook in foundation chain made at the base of the previous dc, yo, pull through, yo, pull through 1 loop and then continue dc as usual. Repeat from * to **continue.**

<u>Joining in new colors</u>-When making the last sc before changing colors, insert hook in stitch, yo and pull through (2 loops on hook). Next, pick up second color, yo and pull through the 2 loops to complete the sc. You are now ready to stitch with the new color. If necessary, carry along the first color by laying the yarn along the top of the previous row and making the sc in the new color around

Materials

Yarn: Fingering or sock weight wool MC: Grey-50g/230yds(210m), CC1: Red-50g/230yds(210m), CC2: Tan-Enough for hooks

Gauge: For cuff-5.5 stitches/in and 3.5 rows/in For glove-6.5 stitches/in and 7 rows/in (2.5 stitches/cm and 2.7 rows/cm)

Hook: 3mm or size needed to obtain gauge

S(M):   Cuff height 2"(2")-5.1(5.1)cm, Cuff circumference 6"(6.5")-15.25(16.5)cm, Glove width at base of thumb 4"(4.25")-10.1(10.8)cm

Top of cuff to top of glove (picots not included) 4"(4.5")-10.1(11.4)cm

Cuff (make two)	
Rnd 1	In MC 34(36) foundation double crochet (fdc). Slip stitch to top of starting chain 3 to join. (Use yarn tail to connect base of chain 3 to base of last fdc.)
Rnd 2	Ch 3, front post double crochet (fpdc) around next stitch, *dc in next st, fpdc around following st. Repeat from * around. Slip stitch to top of ch 3 to join. 34(36) st.
Rnd 3-7	Repeat round 2.
Right Glove (working in rows)	
Row 1	(Increase Row) Ch 2, sc in same st, sc in next 32(34) st, 2 sc in next stitch. Turn. DO NOT JOIN. 36(38) st.
Row 2	Work Even Row) Ch 2, skip 1st sc, sc in next 34(36) st, sc in top of ch 2
Row 3-9	Continue alternating increase and work even rows. 44(46) st in row 9.
Row 10	Ch 2, skip 1st sc, sc in next 17(18) st. Join in CC1, sc in next 3 st (carry along MC under these stitches). Drop CC1 (it will be picked up again when coming back the other way). Pick MC back up and sc in each remaining stitch in row. Turn. 44(46) st
Row 11	Ch 2, sc in same stitch, sc in next 15(16) st. Pick up CC1, sc in next 7 st (carry along MC). Drop CC1. Pick up MC and sc in next 20 st, 2 sc in next st. Turn. 46(48) st
Row 12-18	While still alternating work even and increase rows continue the color work according to chart 1 in the same manner as described above. 52(54) st in row 18.
Size Small Only	
Row 19	Ch 2, skip 1st sc, sc in next 51 st. Turn. 52 st
Row 20	Sl st in 1st 12 st of row 19. Ch 2, sc in next 37 st, sl st to top of ch 2 to join. DO NOT TURN. 38 st
Row 21-27	Ch 2, sc in each st around. Join. 38 st
Row 28	(Optional) Ch 2, sc in next st, ch 3, sl st through the center of the sc just made to attach chain (1 picot st made). *Sc in next 2 st, picot st in 2nd sc. Repeat from * around. Sl st to top of ch 2 to join. 38 sc, 19 picot st

Size Medium Only (right glove)	
Row 21-22	Working alternate increase and work even rows. 58 st in row 22.
Row 23	Sl st in 1st 5 st of row 22. Ch 2, sc in next 41 st, sl st to top of ch 2 to join. DO NOT TURN. 42 st
Row 24-34	Ch 2, sc in each st around. Join. 42 st
Row 35	(Optional) Same as row 28 from size small. 42 sc, 21 picot st
Fasten off. Make Thumb	
Thumb (same for both gloves)	

Stitch together the edges of rows 1-19(22) of the glove.	
Rnd 1	Attach MC to 1st st of the 'thumb hole' next to the top part of the glove, ch 2, sc in next st, sc in next 13(16) st. Sl st to top of ch 2 to join. 15(18) st
Rnd 2	Ch 2, sc in ea sc around. 15(18) st
Rnd 3-4	Repeat round 2. 15(18) st
Size Medium only	
Rnd 5	Repeat round 2. 15(18) st
Fasten Off	

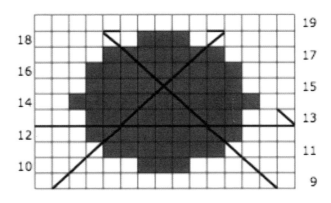

Chart 1: CLF Logo

Left Glove	
Row 1	(Increase row) Ch 2, sc in same st, sc in next 32(34) st, 2 sc in next st. DO NOT JOIN. Turn. 36(38) st
Row 2	(Work Even row) Ch 2, skip 1st sc, sc in next 34(36) st, sc in top of ch 2 from previous row. Turn. 36(38) st.
Row 3-11	Continue alternating increase and work even rows. 46(48) st in row 11.
Row 12	Ch 2, skip 1st sc, sc in next 19(20) st, join in CC1, sc in next 4 st carrying along MC under stitches. Pick up MC, 2 sc carrying along CC1 under stitches. Pick up CC1, 4 sc carrying along MC under stitches. Pick up MC, 2 sc carrying along CC1 under stitches. Pick up CC1, 2 sc carrying along MC under stitches. Drop CC1 (will pick up again when coming back the other way as described for right glove). Pick up MC, 12(13) sc to end of row. Turn. 46(48) st
Row 13-18	While still alternating increase and work even rows, continue the color work according to chart 2. 52(54) st in row 18.
Size Small Only	
Row 19	Ch 2, skip 1st sc, sc in
Row 20	Sl st in 1st 4 st of row 19. Ch 2, sc in next 37 st, sl st to top of ch 2 to join. DO NOT TURN. 38 st
Row 21-27	Ch 2, sc in each st around. Join. 38
Row 28	(Optional) Ch 2, sc in next st, ch 3, sl st through the center of the sc just made to attach chain (1 picot st made). *Sc in next 2 st, picot st in 2nd sc. Repeat from * around. Sl st to top of ch 2 to join. 38 sc, 19 picot st

Row 19-22	Continue working alternate increase and work even rows. 58 st in row 22
Row 23	Sl st in 1st 13 st of row 22. Ch 2, sc in next 41 st, sl st to top of ch 2 to join. DO NOT TURN. 42 st
Row 24-34	Ch 2, sc in each st around. Join. 42 st
Row 35	Optional) Same as row 28 from size small. 42 sc, 21 picot st
Fasten Off. Make Thumb	

FINISHING TOUCHES

Weave in ends.
Embroider hooks onto right glove according to black lines on chart 1 using CC2.
(You may wish to use double thickness yarn so that they show up better.)
Gentle iron or block.

Chart 2: Initials

My Road to Freeform

by Annette Petavy ©2008. Annette Petavy

I have always admired the works of freeform crocheters. The wealth of stitches, the many colors, the ability to create so freely and so profusely have always impressed me. Many times, I have sat down with my box full of left-over partial balls of yarn in dozens of colors and grabbed a hook with the firm intention to create something freeform. But it has never worked.

Sitting there with hook in hand, incapable of producing anything but yet another rectangular swatch of a well known stitch pattern I have often asked myself: "What's wrong?". It can't be lack of creativity – I know that I have loads of that (or I wouldn't be a crochet designer). But my creativity works best when it's framed by some type of structure or plan. When I can create with absolute freedom, I do nothing. It's paralyzing.

Since my response to any problem occurring in my life is to find a book about it, I have several books on freeform. However, I know that sometimes you need to read several books before you find that single and unique book which speaks to you in a way you understand and can apply to your own life. Recently I found such a book, which helped me start on the road to freeform.

It's a self-published book by Myra Wood, called Creative Crochet Lace. I had read about it on various blogs and forums, and finally couldn't resist the temptation. It's not that one more crochet book on my already bulging bookshelves would make a dramatic difference, so why not try this one?

I received the book, and I read. I read, I read and I read. I admired the delicate lace constructions, and decided that the next time I was up to challenging myself with freeform crochet again, it would be with Myra's advice and approach firmly held in mind.

"The next time" arrived pretty soon. I was going to an April wedding, and realized that the chilly spring weather could prove to be incompatible with the relatively light outfit I had chosen to wear. I needed a shawl. The outfit was a lovely coral red, and I didn't have a single matching item in my drawers.

Should I buy a shawl? Buy a shawl??? Should I, a crocheter, go out and buy a shawl which would probably be more expensive and certainly much less interesting and beautiful than anything I could make myself? I just couldn't do it. I had to make it myself. But with just a couple of weeks left to the wedding, I had to make up my mind fast. It couldn't be

So, I pulled out Myra's book again. I decided to give it a go. I paid a visit to my nearest Phildar store, bought a yarn much thicker than I would normally use (I had to consider the time factor) in an off-white colour which didn't clash with the coral red (it was impossible to match the colour). This time of course, it was out of the question to sit there, paralyzed and dumbfounded, incapable of making a stitch. But this time it wouldn't happen. I had a plan...

I went home, and pulled out my favorite stitch dictionaries. They all contain motifs. Typically, I don't design a lot with motifs – which doesn't mean I'm not attracted to them. This was the occasion to try out all the motifs I had lusted for, without being capable of incorporating them into a design.

So, I choose a motif and worked it. When it was completed, I did not fasten off. Instead, I took a deep breath, read a few paragraphs in Creative Crochet Lace to give me strength, and started to work random stitches into the last round of the well-planned, structured motif. It was hard at first, but I kept on it. Double crochets, chain-arches, small clusters... I worked around the motif, I turned around, I exaggerated the motif's shape in one place and evened it out in another. When at last I really didn't know what else to do, I fastened off. I had created a piece of lace fabric, where the center was structured and symmetrical and the edges blurred out into a happy hotch-potch of stitches. In short, I had just taken my first step on the road to freeform. And it was fun! I chose another motif from one of the books, and started all over again.

Slowly, my shawl grew. Very soon, I realized that when joining my lace pieces a new and happy fabric emerged. I filled in holes between pieces with chain arches or small, improvised motifs. Every time I started on a new motif, I was guided by the pattern and could relax into the repetitive music of a well balanced crochet construction. When the motif itself was finished, I could break free and do whatever struck my fancy. Sometimes I didn't finish the last round in the motif, but started to "blur the edges" earlier. Sometimes I just worked the first few rows, to fit into an open space in the fabric which needed filling.
At first, I thought I was making a stole, but it turned out to be a somewhat triangular shawl, which made me think of an irregularly shaped butterfly. Even if I hadn't planned an exact shape or size, I had no problems to decide when I needed to stop – the night before the wedding was my natural deadline.
I couldn't believe my eyes – I had produced a freeform item. Of course, I was eager to show it off the next day, at the wedding which was held in a beautiful medieval castle.
It didn't really turn out as expected. The aperitif was served in an ice-cold wine-cellar. Everyone kept their coat on. And after that, during dinner, I was seated next to the gigantic fire-place, and was very happy not to have chosen a warmer outfit.
That didn't matter. The wedding deadline was just a way to make it happen, to push me out in the wild and try my wings in my own way. My lacey freeform butterfly now exists, and it will be worn on some other occasion. And my hook is itching to take off down the road on a new freeform adventure...

Natcromo Freeform CAL ©2008 KateTorode (aka Kaet)

This game was created in March 2008 on the CLF offshoot celebrating (Inter)National Crochet Month on Ravelry. I'm leaving the March dates in, but obviously this could be done over any 31 days, or all at once, if you prefer. The most important thing is to have fun and enjoy the learning!

Okay, the rules of the game are that every day of March 2008 you will receive two game instructions:
1. a particular stitch to do
2. a change in medium (hook, yarn or direction)

The number of the given stitch to do will be chosen using a given random number generator. If you do not have access to the given generator, please ask a friend for a random number in the given range and do that many of the stitch.

Where a given stitch/pattern name has variations, you should do the variation of your choice. (So DC may be done by either UK or US versions, a shell or fan may have different numbers of stitches within it.) The variation chosen should be consistent on that day. Every stitch should have at least one variation described online, and most will be in any good stitch dictionary.

I am assuming everyone has access to at least two hooks and two yarns. If a given instruction won't work for you (eg I say to go up a hook size and you're already using your largest) please use your discretion.

This is only meant to take a few minutes each day and should not be detrimental to your other projects! I hope it's fun.

March 1 instructions:
Throw a single die and chain that number using your favourite hook
and the brightest available yarn. (ch a number between 1 and 6)

March 2 instructions:
Pick a card from a standard playing pack, and do that number of single crochet with a slightly smaller hook into yesterday's chain. Keep going around the chain in a spiral if today's number is bigger than yesterday's. (Ace=1, Jack=11, Queen=12, King=13, Joker=15 - yes I know 14 is missing, but this is the scoring method my family uses for certain games.)
(sc a number between 1 and 15 into your chain.)

March 3 instructions:
Please change yarn and do treble crochets around your piece. Today's number depends on how many candles you lit last time you did, whether this was for a birthday (doesn't have to be yours), religious reason, dinner party or whatever.
(1+ tr)

March 4 instructions:
Choosing your number from the page you're on of a book or magazine you're currently reading, please change direction and make that number of filet spaces in rows, making every tenth (if there are any) space filled

March 5 instructions:
Going up a hook size or two, do your favourite/lucky number of half-trebles/-doubles. (If you did the filet spaces in rows rather than in the round, please go down the side now, rather than back along the top.)

March 6 instructions:
Change yarn, and then add up all the digits of however many posts you've made on Ravelry's forums (If you aren't on Ravelry use the number of emails you've sent recently). Today we are making a double layer of petals along or around the piece. (If your number was 1, please count this as one pair of petals.)
(2-36 petals in a double layer.)

March 7 instructions:
Change either your yarn or your hook to give you the best comfort, because today we're doing a speed trial. Give yourself 3 minutes to do as many hdc/htr as you can

March 8 instructions:
Changing yarns again, I'm afraid, and we're doing puff stitches today. Please choose the number of the month you were born, and do that many puffs.
(1-12 puff stitches.)

March 9 instructions:
Please change to a smaller hook and depending on what hour of the day it is, do that many fans

March 10 instructions:
After the fans come clusters, in a different yarn, please. This time use the date of the month on which you were born.
(1-31 clusters)

March 11 instructions:
Please add up the digits in the year of your birth, change direction, and do that many extended double (UK)/single (US) crochet stitches.
(2-28 edc/esc)

March 12 instructions:
Please measure the length of your hair in centimetres, and do that many back post trebles, in a new yarn.

March 13 instructions:
Whatever number you would give the day of the week it is today, do that many bullion stitches, with a larger hook.
(1-7 bullions)

March 14 instructions:
Adding up the digits in your telephone number enough times that it becomes reasonable, hold the current yarn together with a previous one and do that many v-stitches.

March 15 instructions:
Using just the newer yarn from yesterday, do front post half doubles/trebles by the number of letters in your online name.

March 16 instructions:
Change direction and do a number of double trebles based on the birth weight of you or your child.

March 17 instructions:
Using a smaller hook, make a ruffled section across a number of stitches based on the number of yarns currently in your project. Put two double crochets in each stitch, and do the same number of rows (still with 2dc in each stitch) as stitches you are originally working across.

This instruction isn't very clear, so the following alternative may help:

1. Change to a smaller hook.
2. Take your number from the number of yarns you have used so far in the piece.
3. You are now going to do double that number of double crochets, 2 in each stitch (so in the number of stitches you got).
4. Turn and do that same number of rows, doubling the number of stitches in each row, by doing two stitches in every stitch.

March 18 instructions:
Change yarn. First do a slip stitch, then a dc/sc, then htr/hdc, then tr/dc, then dtr/tr, and keep stepping up. How tall will you go? Do a second of your tallest stitch, and step all the way down again.

March 19 instructions:
Change hook size, and do spike stitches to the age you started formal education.

March 20 instructions: Time to make some picots, to the number of years of formal education you want to admit to (so far). Then when those are done, please fasten off your yarn. (We'll be picking up elsewhere tomorrow.)	**March 27 instructions:** **Take a larger hook, and do as many X-stitches as there are windows in the house/apartment/building you are currently in**
March 21 instructions: Join a new yarn in on the opposite edge to where you finished yesterday's instruction, and do as many popcorn stitches as you know languages.	**March 28 instructions:** Please change yarn again, and do Astrakhan stitch to the value of the last postage stamp you used.
March 22 instructions: Depending on how many projects you have in your Ravelry notebook, please do that many loop stitches with a larger hook. If you aren't on Ravelry, then do however many you have to hand, finished or not.	**March 29 instructions:** Crab stitch in a larger hook to the number of colours you are wearing.
March 23 instructions: Change yarns, and we're doing the basic Tunisian stitch today. Please flip a coin to do two or three rows of a number of stitches to the value of your coin. (Keep it relatively small and they should fit on a normal crochet hook.)	**March 30 instructions:** Change yarn and do picot crowns to the number of timepieces you use/have changed this month.
March 24 instructions: **Using either a single die with a large number of sides, or multiple dice with 6 sides (or an online equivalent) obtain a number of treble crochets to do, alternately in the front or back loops.**	**March 31 instructions:** Using your favourite hook, take the average age in your household and do that many corkscrew fringes.
March 25 instructions: Based on your most recent game score (if this was very large, add the digits) use a smaller hook and do slip stitches.	Note from the Big Cheese: I asked Kate to send this game for submission into the book. Her brilliant brain child provided many CLF members (and others) with great amusement and wonderful crochet learning opportunities during Inter-NATCROMO!
March 26 instructions: Change yarn, and do Solomon's knot stitches to the first number you look up and see.	

Gallery of Free Form Crochet

Freeform crochet takes many forms:

Top Left: Hat made with wool yarn using plain and relief stitches. Center panel of hat a mohair/shell yarn.

Feathered motif used as embellishment .

Center Top: Free form amulet pouch made with wool/mohair.

Bottom Center: Irish crochet motif made in mohair to be used in a motif shawl. (motifs are a great way to add to your free form!)

Bottom Right: Free form pouch made with acrylic chenille/sari silk yarn. A variety of stitches were used to make the funky Boho pouch.

Right Top: Wool/Alpaca yarn using a variety of stitches to make a **young girl's chapeau.**

Golly's Broomsticks

- a hooded scarf -
Designed by Adrienne Via (aka Grieney)

When my mother asked for a scarf for her birthday, I knew that a hooded scarf would be the perfect solution for a woman who also likes to keep her head warm. The construction of the hood itself creates a smooth profile while the broomstick lace adds an elegant trim to the top and bottom of the garment.   ~ Adrienne Via

Hook: Size **J/10 (6 mm)** *or size to obtain gauge*

Needle: Size **19 (15 mm) knitting needle**

Notions: Yarn needle

Gauge: 11 dcs and 6 rows in scarf pattern = 3"

Difficulty: Medium

**Finished Size: Scarf is about 7" wide and 56" long,
Hood is about 11" deep and 11" tall**

Yarn: BERROCO *Peruvia* (3.5 oz/100 g skeins, each approx 174 yds/160 m; 100% Peruvian Highland Wool): 3 skeins #7143 Aquamarina

Yarn Substitution: About 480 yds/440 m Aran weight yarn

Featured Stitches

flo: front loop only

blo: back loop only

Broomstick Lace: This stitch is performed by pulling loops of yarn to the right side (RS) of the garment and placing them on a 'broomstick', the knitting needle in this case, in order to keep the size of the loops uniform. In the next row, take four loops together and crochet 4 sc across the top, through the center of the loops. Be sure to keep the tension in the loops consistent.

Tip: Stabilize the broomstick by holding it between your knees; this leaves both hands free to work the yarn.

Row 1: With RS facing, *insert hook into next stitch, yo and pull up loop. Enlarge the loop and place it on the broomstick. Repeat from * per pattern directions.

Row 2: *Insert hook through first 4 loops on the broomstick, yo and draw through all 4 loops, yo and pull through both loops on hook (first sc made). Work 3 more sc in group, rep from * with the next four loops on the broomstick per pattern directions.

Scarf

To begin: Ch 201.

Hood

This section refers to three groups of stitches: hood stitches (hdcs and dcs), scarf stitches and the scs that join the hood to the scarf. Note that no stitches are worked into the top of the scs.

	Scarf		Hood
Row 1	Sc in second ch from hook and in each chain across, turn.		Ch 20.
Row 2	Ch 3 (counts as first dc here and throughout), dc in each sc across, turn.	*Row 1*	With RS facing, sc in middle st of scarf Row 11 (st #100, counting from the right-hand side) and sc in next scarf stitch (#101), turn, ch 1, sc back along the ch, 4 sc in last ch st, then sc down the other side of the ch in each st towards scarf, sc in next two scarf sts (#99 and 98), turn.
Row 3	Ch 1, sc in each of first 2 dc, sl st into next dc so that this loop is pulled towards the front (RS) of the scarf, enlarge loop and place it on the broomstick, *insert hook into next dc from front to back, pull up loop towards the front of the scarf and place it on the broomstick, rep from * across to last 2 scs, sl st into next sc, ch 1, sc in same st, sc in last st, turn. [2 sc, 196 loops, 2 sc]	*Row 2*	Hdc in last hood stitch of previous row, dc blo in next 16 sts, (2 dc blo in next st, dc blo in next 2 sts) 3 times, dc blo in next 16 sts, hdc in last st, sc in next two scarf sts, turn
Row 4	Ch 3, dc in next sc, *insert hook through first 4 loops on	*Row 3*	Hdc in last hood stitch of previous row,

broomstick, yo and draw through all 4 loops, yo and draw though both loops on hook (first sc made), work 3 more sc into center of loops, rep from * for the rest of the loops, dc in last two sts, turn. [200 sts]

dc flo in next 17 sts, (2 dc flo in next st, dc flo in next 2 sts) 4 times, dc flo in next 16 sts, hdc in last st, sc in next two scarf sts, turn.

Row 5 Ch 3, dc flo in next st and in each st across, turn.	**Row 4** Hdc in last hood stitch of previous row, dc blo in next 17 sts, (2 dc blo in next st, dc blo in next 2 sts) 5 times, dc blo in next 17 sts, hdc in last st, sc in next two scarf sts,, turn.
Row 6 to 11 Rep Row 5, fasten off at end of Row 11.	**Row 5** Hdc in last hood stitch of previous row, dc flo in next 18 sts, (2 dc flo in next st, dc flo in next 2 sts) 6 times, dc flo in next 18 sts, hdc in last st, sc in next two scarf sts,, turn.

Hood Continued

Row 6 Hdc in last hood stitch of previous row, dc blo in next 20 sts, (2 dc blo in next st, dc blo in next 2 sts) 7 times, dc blo in next 19 sts, hdc in last st, sc in next two scarf sts, turn.

Row 7 Hdc in last hood stitch of previous row, dc flo in next 28 sts, (2 dc flo in next st, dc flo in next 3 sts) 3 times, dc flo in next 27 sts, hdc in last st, sc in next two scarf sts, turn.

Row 8 Hdc in last hood stitch of previous row, dc blo in next 68 sts, hdc in last st, sc in next two scarf sts, turn

Row 9 Hdc in last hood stitch of previous row, dc flo in next 68 sts, hdc in last st, sc in next two scarf sts, turn.

Row 10 thru 15 Rep rows 8 and 9 three times.

Row 16 Hdc in last hood stitch of previous row, dc blo in next 68 sts, hdc in last st, sc in next scarf stitch, fasten off.

Top Trim		Row 3	Ch 3, dc flo in each st across, turn. [228]
Row 1	(WS) Starting at the far left end of the scarf, join yarn with sl st in first dc, ch 1, sc in next st, sl st into next dc, enlarge loop and place it on the broomstick, *insert hook into next dc, pull up loop and place it on the broomstick, rep from * across to last scarf st, sc in last scarf st and in first 3 hood sts, sl st into next hood dc, enlarge loop and place it on the broomstick, *insert hook into next dc, pull up loop and place it on the broomstick, rep from * across to last 3 hood sts, sc in last three hood sts and first two scarf sts, sl st into next scarf dc, enlarge loop and place it on the broomstick, *insert hook into next dc, pull up loop and place it on the broomstick, rep from * across to last 2 scarf st, sc in last two scarf sts, do not turn. [2 sc, 80 lps, 4 sc, 64 loops, 5 sc, 80 loops, 2 sc]	Row 4	Ch 1, sc in each st across, fasten off. [228]
Row 2	Ch 3, dc in next sc, *insert hook through first 4 loops on broomstick, yo and draw through all 4 loops, yo and draw though both loops on hook (first sc made), work 3 more sc into center of loops, rep from * for the rest of the loops (ignore the scs between loop groups), dc in last two sts, turn. [2 dc, 224 sc, 2 dc].	Finishing	Weave in loose ends. Steam gently to block, if desired.

Adrienne Via lives in Columbia, MD, where she tries to convert the knitters in her weekly group. She thanks Amy for showing her the difference between a slip stitch and a single crochet, Jeff for his photography and enthusiasm for all things crafty, her beagle Jake for never eating her crochet hooks, and Maura, Sarah and Swapna for their patience.

The Makings of a Crochet Group
by Tracie Neill (Mscrochets)

When I joined the Crochet Guild of America, I did so with the intent of finding other crocheters in my area, only to learn that there weren't many, at least not in the Guild. I was disappointed to realize there wasn't even a chapter in my area, nor any other kind of crochet group–except for a knitting group that "welcomed" crocheters. I went a couple of times, but being the only one yielding a hook, I decided it wasn't for me. Too, I really wanted more than a chat and stitch group; I wanted to make a difference in the community with crochet, as well as host workshops, discussions, teaching sessions, and engage in any other outlet for my skills I could find. So instead of sitting, waiting, and wishing, I decided to do something about it. That's when a crochet-specific group was born in my area.

If you've run into a similar dilemma, why not tackle it the same why by beginning your own group? I'm not going to say it'll be an easy task, but it won't be impossible either, and with the following pointers, you'll be well on your way to hanging out with the hooking crowd in your own area. It may seem like a lot of work, but starting a crochet group is rewarding and well worth the effort.

- **Starting and maintaining** a group will require some time and energy, so first off decide how much of each you can and are willing to devote to the birth and growth of this venture. You may have to *make* the time depending on how busy your schedule is and how badly you really want to be the one to get the ball of yarn rolling. This should be thought of as a long-term commitment. Don't get people excited then leave them to congregate on their own. That's not to say that later down the line you can't step down, but you should make the initial commitment to do what is necessary to keep the group going for the long haul, even during the slow times–and there *will* be slow times.
- Next, **decide what it is that you want in a crochet-related group in your area**. Do you just want to get together with others to crochet and chat? Or do you want to do some charity crochet work and host events? Do you want to be informal or formal? Election of officers is optional, but if you choose to be a formal group, it may be the way to go. Figuring out your own reasons for wanting a crochet-specific group is an important first step in its creation and will help you determine which direction you want to take it.(One thing I noticed when my group was first starting, several people expressed a desire to crochet for local charities, which has been incorporated into our meeting schedule, and it seems to be the main attraction for several of our members.)
- **Do you want your group to have any affiliation with the CGOA** (Crochet Guild of America)? If so, at least one member of your group has to be a member of the Guild. The advantage to this type of affiliation is that you can get your group listed with the Guild, which in turn will put you in touch with others in and around your area, no matter how few or great those numbers are, including other chapters that may be close but too far to travel to. Too, it gives you a backbone for your group, keeps you in the know as to events hosted by the Guild, and they also offer some tips as to how to get a group started, as well as some ideas for various crochet-related programs. (To find out more, go to http://crochet.org.)
- **Find a wing-(wo)man--someone who is as excited about crochet** as you are and is willing to help you make some of the first decisions concerning the group. You'll also want this person to be someone who can take over in case you can't attend a meeting or event or any other place where your presence may be important, especially if you choose not to elect officers. You may not meet this person until after your first couple of meetings; just be open to a new friend if you don't have one already willing to help.

- **Decide what defines a member of your group**. How do you determine who is and who isn't a member? Some groups charge membership dues and the perks to go along with them, which determines if someone is a member or not. For this kind of group, you'll need to check into what is required in order to receive dues and for keeping up with how the money is spent, such as opening a checking account and electing a treasurer. If you don't want to charge dues, then think about what other characteristics membership would be compiled of. Regulars to the meetings might be considered the "true" members, while those who visit on occasion may just be considered visitors, and if you're smart, visitors are always welcome. Some clubs who charge membership dues also charge visitors per each visit. Have those who wish to be considered members fill out a contact form that you can keep on file for your own personal reference. You may also want to compile a member list to share with the group, but seek permission from each member as to what information they want made available. What is considered a member or not a member is totally up to you and those in the group, depending on how formal or informal the group is. You may start out not charging dues, then later, once your group is established and you have perks to being a member, you can then do what it takes to be a due-required group. If you aren't charging dues, you can ask members to volunteer to help with expenses for running the group. Have those who want things mailed to them via snail mail bring their own self-addressed stamped envelopes. Ask if anyone would like to make copies of any materials you might use for a meeting or for advertising the group. Don't be shy about seeking and accepting the help of others.

- **Find a place to host the first and future meetings**. This may sound like a really easy thing to do, but depending on where you live, it could prove to be one of the most difficult tasks in the beginning. Check with your public library and see if they have meeting rooms available. It's possible they do and for non-profits, they may not charge a fee. (My library even lists our meetings on their board of events which are located in several places within the facility.) Another idea would be to write or email your chamber of commerce for a list of possible meeting places in the area. Churches, community buildings, a local yarn store, coffee shops, bookstores–these are all good places to check for space. You probably want a place you can use for free, unless you plan to charge dues and use the money to rent the space. You also want a place that is easily accessible by everyone. Keep it public since most people are more comfortable in well-established places in their community rather than in a stranger's home. The first meeting may be at one place until you know what other options are available and/or what works for those who join, but it's important to the growth of the group to find a meeting space for the long-term.

- **Decide on a time schedule** that works well for you, but be as flexible as possible. What may work for you, may or may not work for many others. Do you want this new group to meet every week? Once a month? In the morning, the afternoon, or evening? Once a day or twice a day? Some groups meet once a month on the same date, but at two different times such as morning and evening, so they can accommodate the most people. Others meet one or two Sunday afternoons per month or on the same night every week. Once you know what works well for you, you'll want to find out what works well for everyone else. Ask everyone for their input during the first meeting and get things established shortly afterwards. You can always add more meeting times later on, but try to get a set schedule going as soon as possible so others can plan around it.

- **Talk to others who lead** and/or attend crochet guilds and find out what works for them. The more ideas you have, the better prepared you will be for forming and maintaining your own group. Every group is different, so it's important to find what works best for the group in your area and use that as a foundation for building your own group upon.
- **Figure out a name** for the group–something catchy but easy to for people to remember. If you can't come up with a name, you can always wait until the first meeting and let others help decide on one.

- **Understand that not everyone is computer-literate,** nor do they want to be. Those who have been crocheting for more years than you can imagine possibly do not have a computer and really don't want to be part of anything that is on the internet. Thus, it's important to accommodate those by keeping them in the loop verbally at meetings or through snail mail, rather than expecting everyone to access information through email or online forums.
- **Ideas for meetings are as vast as crochet is versatile,** but to get you started, here are a few suggestions: <u>Crochet and Chat</u> - Just what the name implies. <u>Show 'n Share</u> - Allow time for members to show off and talk about their latest projects. <u>Help Session</u> - Encourage members to seek help with a pattern or stitch that may be causing them some problems. <u>Workshops</u> - Teach a new technique yourself or have another member do so. <u>Crochet Alongs</u> - Have everyone work on the same project then see how they all differ when the projects are completed. <u>Charity Crochet</u> - Set time aside, perhaps an entire meeting per month, to work on projects to donate.

- You're now getting your hooks all in a row, and are ready to prepare for that first of many meetings. Advertise your meeting, even if it's just letting a forum or two know of your beginnings. Talk it up amongst your crochet friends and on online message boards that have crochet-related topics. Create fliers to distribute in prominent places in your community, such as craft and yarn stores or on a localized bulletin board. Make an outline or a handout to distribute at the initial meeting of your thoughts and ideas about what you want for the group as a whole. Include your own vision for the group, as well as what kinds of things you plan for this group to be a part of. Define your idea of what constitutes a member and what doesn't, and ask for opinions and thoughts on the topic. You may also want to come up with a worksheet of questions for those who attend the first couple of meetings to gain an idea as to what others want in a group such as this. Ask for help in deciding on a meeting place and schedule that works for you and the majority of those that want to be involved. It's important to note that consistency in where you meet and what time is crucial to keeping the group running smoothly. If you only meet sporadically, it will be more difficult, if not impossible, for others to keep up with what's going on, and it will also make the group appear to be flaky. Be willing to compromise some, but **never** give up on your own vision. It is, after all, what has brought you to this point thus far.
- Offer opportunities for others to share their knowledge with the group. The group shouldn't be a "me, my, and mine" based one. Without others joining and taking part, there won't be a group, now matter how much time and effort you put into starting one. You should not only be a leader, but also be a follower when necessary. Encourage members to lead a workshop in an area of expertise they are comfortable with teaching. Ask for volunteers when they are needed. Assign committees. You don't know if you don't ask, and some may not be comfortable with speaking up, especially in the beginning stages. Don't try to make all of the decisions on your own. Express your desires to those who attend your meetings and let everyone help make some of the tough decisions. Get as many people involved as is needed and is possible.

- As a group, be active in the community by not only crocheting for charities, but by participating in walks with a cause in your area, or by teaching crochet in a nursing home or to school-aged children. Host a crochet-out. Read a novel with a crochet topic as a group, then host a book review. There are so many possibilities for being more than just a crochet and chat group for those who want to be and do more. Of course, just chatting with others while you crochet is fun, too, but being a part of the community will open other doors for sharing your love of crochet with those outside your newly-formed circle of friends and it will expand the group's sense of purpose.
- You should now be well on your way to success. But there's more. Once you have all of your specifics set in stone–when, where, why, and how–start doing some major advertising for your group to gain more attention. Create and distribute a brochure, design and maintain a web site, start a blog and let other members help write for it, begin a newsletter, and open a members-only message board where your members can have access to important club information that isn't meant to be public. Check with your local newspaper and see if they have a free listing of clubs and meetings both online and in print. Make business cards with your information to hand out to strangers you meet at craft and yarn stores. Don't hesitate to offer an invitation to someone who is crocheting in public. Invite anyone and everyone you think would be interested. Talk it up. It's very possible that there are many around you who have wanted to be a part of a crochet group for a long time but never knew how to get one started or didn't have the time to, and are now overjoyed to see someone take the yarn by the hook.

Most of all, have fun, and Happy Crocheting!

Crochet Dragon Scale Socks

By Jenniffer Reeve (aka Craftkitten)

Instructions: Women's Size- 6/7 US or 38/39 EU

Materials: approximately 400/450/500 yds sock yarn. Size D 3.25mm hook. 1 locking stitch marker.(I used 3 balls of Crystal Palace -Panda Silk, [50gr, 204 yds per ball. 52% Bamboo, 43% Superwash merino wool, 5% combed silk.]

Gauge: In hdc: 8sts & 5 rows to 1 inch, In pattern stitch: 1 fan= ¾ of an inch and 3 Rounds = 1 inch

Note: *Sock is worked from the toe, up with an "afterthought heel". The toe and heel are worked in a spiral with no turning ch. (Heel instructions for all sizes found in final section of pattern instructions)*

Rnd 1	**2 hdc in 3rd ch from hook, 1 hdc in each of next 4 ch, 4 hdc in last ch, working on other side of chain, 1 hdc in each of next 4 ch, 2 hdc in first ch of rnd.**	16 sts
Rnd 2	Work in hdc around, working 2 hdc twice on each side with 6 sts between increases. Mark 1st increase as beginning of round on this and each successive round. *This is to compensate for the twisting or "procession" of the rounds.*	20 sts
Rnd 3	Hdc around, working 2 hdc twice on each side with 8 sts between increases.	24 sts
Rnd 4	Hdc around, working 2 hdc twice on each side with 10 sts between increases.	28 sts
Rnd 5	Hdc around, working 2 hdc twice on each side with 12 sts between increases.	32 sts
Rnd 6	Hdc around, working 2 hdc twice on each side with 14 sts between increases.	36 sts
Rnd 7	Hdc around, working 2 hdc twice on each side with 16 sts between increases.	40 sts
Rnd 8	Hdc around, working 2 hdc twice on each side with 18 sts between increases.	44 sts
Rnd 9	Hdc around, working 2 hdc twice on each side with 20 sts between increases.	48 sts
Rnds 10-14	Work even. At end of rnd 14, turn work inside out.	48 sts
Rnd 15	Sc in next st, turn, ch 1, sc in same st, [sk 3 st, 7 dc in next st, sk 3 st, sc in next st] repeat around, join with slst to first sc.	48 sts

Rnd 16	Ch 3, 3 dc in same st, sk 3 st, sc in next st, [sk 3 st, 7 dc in next st, sk 3 st, sc in next st] repeat around, ending with 3 dc in same st as ch 3, join with slst to top of ch 3.	48 sts
Rnd 17	Ch 1, sc in same st, [sk 3 st, 7 dc in next st, sk 3 st, sc in next st] repeat around, join with slst to first sc.	48 sts
Rnds 18-27	Rep rnds 16-17. *Sock has reached the highest part of the arch, about 7 " from toe tip.*	48 sts
Rnd 28 Increase rnd	Ch 3, 3 dc in same st, sk 3 st, sc in next st (sk 1 st, 7 dc in next st, sk 1 st, sc in next st) 4 times, [sk 3 st, sc in next st, sk 3 st, 7 dc in next st, sk 3 st, sc in next st] around, ending with 3 dc in same st as ch 3, join with slst to top of ch 3. *Increases should be on the sole of the sock.*	64 sts
Rnds 29-35	Rep rnds 16-17 as applicable. *Sock has reached the beginning of the heel pad – for a total length about 2 " less than the total length of the sock.*	64 sts
Heel split	Ch 31, sk 4 fans, join to next sc.	
Rnd 36	Work as in Rnd 16, working into chains where applicable.	64 sts
Rnd 37-58	Rep rnds 16-17 as applicable. Continue to desired length.	64 sts

Women' Size- 8/9 US or 40/41 EU to begin: Ch 8

Rnd 1	**2 hdc in 3rd ch from hook, 1 hdc in each of next 4 ch, 4 hdc in last ch, working on other side of chain, 1 hdc in each of next 4 ch, 2 hdc in first ch of rnd.**	**16 sts**
Rnd 2	Work in hdc around, working 2 hdc twice on each side with 6 sts between increases. Mark 1st increase as beginning of round on this and each successive round. *This is to compensate for the twisting or "procession" of the rounds.*	20 sts
Rnd 3	Hdc around, working 2 hdc twice on each side with 8 sts between increases.	24 sts
Rnd 4	Hdc around, working 2 hdc twice on each side with 10 sts between increases.	28 sts
Rnd 5	Hdc around, working 2 hdc twice on each side with 12 sts between increases.	32 sts
Rnd 6	Hdc around, working 2 hdc twice on each side with 14 sts between increases.	36 sts
Rnd 7	Hdc around, working 2 hdc twice on each side with 16 sts between increases.	40 sts
Rnd 8	Hdc around, working 2 hdc twice on each side with 18 sts between increases.	44 sts
Rnd 9	Hdc around, working 2 hdc twice on each side with 20 sts between increases.	48 sts
Rnd 10	Hdc around, working 2 hdc twice on each side with 22 sts between increases.	52 sts
Rnd 11	Hdc around, working 2 hdc twice on each side with 24 sts between increases.	56 sts
Rnd 15	Sc in next st, turn, ch 1, sc in same st, [sk 3 st, 7 dc in next st, sk 3 st, sc in next st] repeat around, join with slst to first sc.	56 sts
Rnd 16	Ch 3, 3 dc in same st, sk 3 st, sc in next st, [sk 3 st, 7 dc in next st, sk 3 st, sc in next st] repeat around, ending with 3 dc in same st as ch 3, join with slst to top of ch 3.	56 sts
Rnd 17	Ch 1, sc in same st, [sk 3 st, 7 dc in next st, sk 3 st, sc in next st] repeat around, join with slst to first sc.	56 sts
Rnds 18-30	Rep rnds 16-17 as applicable. *Sock has reached the highest part of the arch, about 8 " from toe tip.*	56 sts
Rnd 31	Ch 1, sc in same st, sk 3 st, sc in next st, 7 dc in next st, sk 3 st, sc in next st (sk 1 st, 7	72 sts

Increase rnd	dc in next st, sk 1 st, sc in next st) 4 times, [sk 3 st, sc in next st, sk 3 st, 7 dc in next st, sk 3 st, sc in next st] around, join with slst to first sc. *Increases should be on the sole of the sock.*	
Rnds 31-37	Rep rnds 16-17 as applicable. *Sock has reached the beginning of the heel pad – for a total length about 2 " less than the total length of the sock.*	72 sts
Heel split	Slst across 1 fan (loosely!), Ch 31, sk 4 fans, join to next sc.	
Rnd 38	Work as in Rnd 16, working into chains where applicable.	72 sts
Rnd 39-60	Rep rnds 16-17 as applicable. Continue to desired length.	72 sts

Women' Size- 10/11 US or 42/43 EU

Ch 8

Rnd 1	**2 hdc in 3rd ch from hook, 1 hdc in each of next 4 ch, 4 hdc in last ch, working on other side of chain, 1 hdc in each of next 4 ch, 2 hdc in first ch of rnd.**	**16 sts**
Rnd 2	Work in hdc around, working 2 hdc twice on each side with 6 sts between increases. Mark 1st increase as beginning of round on this and each successive round. *This is to compensate for the twisting or "procession" of the rounds.*	20 sts
Rnd 3	Hdc around, working 2 hdc twice on each side with 8 sts between increases.	24 sts
Rnd 4	Hdc around, working 2 hdc twice on each side with 10 sts between increases.	28 sts
Rnd 5	Hdc around, working 2 hdc twice on each side with 12 sts between increases.	32 sts
Rnd 6	Hdc around, working 2 hdc twice on each side with 14 sts between increases.	36 sts
Rnd 7	Hdc around, working 2 hdc twice on each side with 16 sts between increases.	40 sts
Rnd 8	Hdc around, working 2 hdc twice on each side with 18 sts between increases.	44 sts
Rnd 9	Hdc around, working 2 hdc twice on each side with 20 sts between increases.	48 sts
Rnd 10	Hdc around, working 2 hdc twice on each side with 22 sts between increases.	52 sts
Rnd 11	Hdc around, working 2 hdc twice on each side with 24 sts between increases.	56 sts
Rnd 12	Hdc around, working 2 hdc twice on each side with 26 sts between increases.	60 sts
Rnds 13-15	Work even. At end of rnd 15, turn work inside out.	60 sts
Rnd 16	Sc in next st, turn, ch 1, sc in same st, [sk 3 st, 7 dc in next st, sk 3 st, sc in next st] repeat around, join with slst to first sc.	60 sts
Rnd 17	Ch 3, 3 dc in same st, sk 3 st, sc in next st, [sk 3 st, 7 dc in next st, sk 3 st, sc in next st] repeat around, ending with 3 dc in same st as ch 3, join with slst to top of ch 3.	60 sts
Rnd 18	Ch 1, sc in same st, [sk 3 st, 7 dc in next st, sk 3 st, sc in next st] repeat around, join with slst to first sc.	60 sts
Rnds 19-30	Rep rnds 17-18. *Sock has reached the highest part of the arch, about 8" from toe tip.*	60 sts
Rnd 31 **Increase rnd**	Ch 3, 3 dc in same st, sk 3 st, sc in next st, sk 3 st, 7 dc in next st, sk 3 st, sc in next st, (sk 1 st, 7 dc in next st, sk 1 st, sc in next st) 4 times, [sk 3 st, sc in next st, sk 3 st, 7 dc in next st, sk 3 st, sc in next st] around, ending with 3 dc in same st as ch 3, join with slst to top of ch 3. *Increases should be on the sole of the sock.*	76 sts
Rnds 32-40	Rep rnds 17-18 as applicable. *Sock has reached the beginning of the heel pad – for a*	76 sts

total length about 2 " less than the total length of the sock.

Heel split	Slst past 2 fans (loosely!), Ch 31, sk 4 fans, join to next sc.	
Rnd 41	Work as in Rnd 17, working into chains where applicable.	76 sts
Rnd 42-62	Rep rnds 1 7-18 as applicable. Continue to desired length.	76 sts

<u>Heel : All Sizes</u>

Turn sock inside out. Join with slst to dc 2 sts to the left from bottom right corner. Mark the beginning of each rnd.

Rnd 1	**Hdc in same st as join and in each of the next 26 sts, hdc2tog,(then on other side) hdc2tog, hdc in each of next 27 sts, hdc2tog,(then on other side) hdc2tog. Do not join.**	**58 sts**
Rnd 2	Hdc in each of the next 26 sts, hdc2tog,(then on other side) hdc2tog, hdc in each of next 25 sts, hdc2tog,(then on other side) hdc2tog. (This actually works into the 1st hdc)	55sts
Rnd 3	Hdc in each of the next 23 sts, hdc2tog,(then on other side) hdc2tog, hdc in each of next 23 sts, hdc2tog,(then on other side) hdc2tog, hdc in last st.	50 sts

Irish Revolution - a lifetime of Crochet

By Orla Breslin (aka Stitchlily)

I don't know whether it's me revolving my life around crochet or it revolving around me. Whatever way it is, it's a curious bond that has been there my whole life. My hooks ARE the security blanket from my past. Well, they are a means to making a security blanket any time I want.

Let's begin at the beginning. I come from a country known for its crochet, Ireland, of course. Where else but here would you find women masochistic enough to do the most detailed of fine lace in bad light and damp cold with arthritic fingers. (An English man living in Ireland for years, noted this trait, he thought most Irish women had it, to prove his point, he told me a joke, "How many Irish Women does it take to change a light bulb?", and of course the answer is "none", because she'll say "It's okay deary, I don't want to put you to any trouble, I'll just sit here in the dark"). I've tried doing lace, and just don't get it; I like fiddlie but not that miniature. My Gran loved it, however.

She was a proper Gran, not these trendy, globetrotting botox nanas of today. Her main sitting room was dark, full of furniture you were scared to sit on, lace doilies, cushion covers everywhere. And yes, she had the toilet dollies, the tissue-covers, the shawls. What a Gran! At the time I didn't appreciate her, she was just old and fidgety, like old people were back then. But now when I think back on those memories, it's all the crochet work that I remember the most, the vast, colourful quantities of it. And it's a warm fuzzy feeling, of a woman who worked hard raising 12 children and STILL managed to make a crochet cover for everything in the house! We think we have it bad…

My first attempt at crochet was learning in school, we made lots and lots of Granny Squares, which were sewn up by mums and grans into clothes for the" *starving babies."* I italic this because, Irish people from birth are filled with this sense of duty, a need to feed and clothe the world. I doubt any of the "starving babies" appreciated these horrendous, scratchy, badly made cardigans, but our intentions were good. So, I fell in love with crochet. I discovered I had something in common with my Gran that was mine alone, that was special. All my aunts knitted, and my sisters did nothing woolly. My special bond, I'm sorry to say was short-lived, for she popped her clogs, died that is. (I just made that up to make myself feel like I had a special bond, I don't remember if I had a special bond or not, before she died, I like to think if she had lived a bit longer, I would have had a special bond). The bond I had with my Gran, and still have, was that I inherited her prize crochet hooks. I'm not sure whether they are bone or ivory, brought back from Africa by an uncle along with an elephant's foot (okay for the sake of trying to regain my pc-ness about the hooks and the elephants foot. In brief, the uncle shot a wild, injured, ransacking elephant, and the villagers were so grateful they gave him the foot made into a table as a present. And as a vegetarian, I had issues with the bone hooks, but if you have ever used these beautiful hand-carved tools, it's impossible to go back to metal or plastic. I'd rather appreciate and use them, than have them sit in a drawer, an animal's life wasted. So thank you animal whoever you were, I really do love them). Enough about my Gran, this is supposed to be my story. Anyway, I got her crochet hooks, which I adore.

So, I kept on crocheting bits and bobs, much to the merriment of my five sisters (I know big family, I am Irish, after all). How they jeered, how my friends thought it was strange. Well, everyone thought it was strange, because in those days 70's and 80's nobody in Ireland made stuff. Except the German hippies living up the mountains au natural.

I kept going because it was my salvation, my way of escaping. In some ways I think it's what got me through my teenage years relatively unharmed, although that has been disputed. Crochet became my way of rebelling. How could my mum seriously give out to me, when I was in my room listening to evil punk music and crocheting? They just didn't seem to go together, but fellow crocheters, we know better don't we! It was like an underground movement, where I was its only member, and I was special. But I was poor. And that, as all teenagers know is a downer, poverty is depressing.

So using my secret hook knowledge, I tried to start funding my burgeoning drinking habit by using my skills. I crocheted mad colourful hats for the hippies, plain ones for the mods and skinheads, spiky ones for the punks. I crocheted large cobwebs for the Goths and cureheads. I swapped hats for pints, and enjoyed my coming of age. My apologies to any non-drinking hookers, I mean crocheters out there, if my crochet driven, drink fueled youth offends you. But that's how it was in Ireland in the 80's/90's. I used to make Christmas presents for my family, until one year my sister asked me not to make her anything, and would I not just buy her something. How offended I was, I still to this day make very little for my family, although now it's back in fashion, and they ask me for things, I say no...

Turning into my twenties, I still had never met anyone else who crocheted. That always amazes me, because of the versatility of this craft. How could anyone consciously choose to knit instead of crochet? It has baffled me all my life, I felt like I was on a life-long failing campaign to further the cause and recruit hookers, and although I have taught many people to crochet, I don't think anyone took it up to any great extent. Anyway, back to my twenties…I crocheted blankets, bags, baby clothes. My few attempts at clothes were complete disasters, just not my thing. I've crocheted wall hangings, flowers, strange shapes. I never knew where all this was coming from, or going to. I was obsessed. Eventually, I decided to go to college, and did a two year course in Textiles. I learnt many new skills, and became obsessed with many other textile techniques. I felted, wove, and yes knitted. (I had too, I got a job in a knitting company, which meant I had to knit, but I got to crochet the hems at least.) I neglected my art, and was distracted by other colourful woolly things.

So, for my late twenties, I have to admit I didn't crochet much. It was a dark period in my life and I have nothing in double, treble, or any other stitch, to show for it, I can only look back in regret. If only I'd known across the waters, in the land of the free, well, any other land but this Celtic consumer-mad society, there was a re-emergence of this forgotten craft. That there were others out there like me. Why in god's name didn't anyone tell me about the internet! I just thought it was full of geeky, game stuff that my geeky, game-playing boyfriend was into. It was only when I got pregnant, and moped around the house bored because I was tired and big and couldn't walk further that 5 steps away from the toilet without panicking (lots of kidney trouble), that I really checked out the internet. I then found patterns for DNA strands, mobieus strips, hyperbolic coral reefs, amigurami animals, and OH MY GOD, *Ravelry*. How could this world exist without me knowing about it, being a part of it?

So now, I'm in my early (fast-approaching middle) thirties and much to the annoyance of my boyfriend and probable my son, I crochet rather than do the housework, I Ravelry rather than cuddle up on the couch. I try to explain in forceful terms; "Don't you know there's a revolution out there?"
It may be slow to hit Ireland, but it's coming. And when it does I want to be the first to stand on the beaches and say "Welcome Crochet Liberation Front, I have been planning and plotting, waiting for your arrival for years. I always knew you would come, and release me from these heathen knitters". **(To be PC again, my apologies to any knitters of strong faith)

Granite To Go
By Mary Zeman

A felted, mid-size bag recipe in a fun, granite stitch and super bulky yarn.

Yarn: Artful Yarns Museum, or other super bulky "6" 100% wool yarn, 3 skeins (about 250 yards) Color of sample: Zanzibar, color 9. Hook: Q Gauge: not critical Felted dimensions, 12" W, 8" high, 2" deep Sk= skip

Ch 38, loosely

1. Sc into 2nd chain from hook, *ch1, sk1, sc into next chain* across, end with sc. Ch1, turn
2. *Sk sc, sc into ch1 sp, ch1* across, sc in last sc. Ch1 turn Repeat rows 1 and 2 until piece meas ures 28-30 inches long. Finish off.

Ch 120 loosely for the strap. Sc in 2nd chain from hook, all the way down, 3sc in last chain, turn, sc back along the other side of the starting chain, 2sc in last chain, join with sl to first sc, finish off.

Fold 1/3 of body of bag up on itself. Using the same yarn, and sc, attach the strap to the bag, such that the strap forms the sides of the bag. Be careful not to twist strap. Finish off.

Felt the bag in hot water, according to general felting instructions.

Check occasionally for desired density, and to keep strap from tangling.

Stuff to desired shape and let dry.

Variations: at one end on the last row, hold a strand of eyelash or novelty yarn with the wool for a fun flap; embellish with buttons. To make a deeper bag, add 1 or more rounds to the strap directions.

Materials:

- worsted weight yarn in two colors (100 yds each for adult hat)
- Size H crochet hook
- Tapestry needle for weaving in ends
- Stitch marker (optional)

Size	last inc rnd
Todder	10
Youth	12

I discovered this deceptively simple stripe pattern while making Easter baskets for my kids in 2007. The beanie is worked in two colors, but only one color per round. After the opening round, the hat is worked in continuous rounds. The beanie may be finished off with a round of shells and a flower embellishment, or by working last 4 rounds in same color. Pattern is written for a snug fit, but is easily adapted to make the hat in a variety of sizes by either doing more or fewer rounds of increases before working even. Stitches are made by working 1 sc and 1 ch into the ch-1 space of the row below; increases are done by working a sc, ch1 into the specified sc of the row below; pattern written so that increases are all done in same color, but can be worked in either color as necessary.

To change colors at end of round: after last sc, bring color A to front, insert hook in next ch 1 space, yarn over with color B, pull through loop on hook, bring color A to back, and proceed with sc in color B. (Pattern written in US terminology).

Round	Color	
1	A	ch3, work 10 dc into 1st chain, close w/ sl st in top of 1st dc
2	A	ch1, *sc, 1ch in each dc around, ending w sc, then with color B, ch1
3	B	*sc, 1ch in next ch-1sp, rep from * around, ending with sc in B, ch1 in A
4	A	*sc, 1ch in next ch-1sp, sc 1ch in next sc; rep from * around, end w/ sc in A and ch 1 in B
5	B	*sc, 1ch in next ch-1sp, rep from * around, ending with sc in B, ch1 in A
6	A	*(sc, 1ch in next ch-1sp) twice, sc 1ch in next sc; rep from * around, end w/ sc in A and ch 1 in B
7	B	*sc, 1ch in next ch-1sp, rep from * around, ending with sc in B, ch1 in A
8	A	*(sc, 1ch in next ch-1sp) three times, sc 1ch in next sc; rep from * around, end w/ sc in A and ch 1 in B
9	B	*sc, 1ch in next ch-1sp, rep from * around, ending with sc in B, ch1 in A
10	A	*(sc, 1ch in next ch-1sp) five times, sc 1ch in next sc; rep from * around, end w/ sc in A and ch 1 in B
11	B	*sc, 1ch in next ch-1sp, rep from * around, ending with sc in B, ch1 in A
12	A	*(sc, 1ch in next ch-1sp) six times, sc 1ch in next sc; rep from * around, end w/ sc in A and ch 1 in B
13	B	*sc, 1ch in next ch-1sp, rep from * around, ending with sc in B, ch1 in A
14	A	*(sc, 1ch in next ch-1sp) seven times, sc 1ch in next sc; rep from * around, end w/ sc in A and ch 1 in B

Part B work even repeating rows 15 &16

15	B	*sc, 1ch in next ch-1sp, rep from * around, ending with sc in B, ch1 in A
16	A	*sc, 1ch in next ch-1sp, rep from * around, ending with sc in A, ch1 in B

17	choice	ch1, *work 5 dc into next ch1 space, skip next ch1 space, sc in next ch1 space; rep from * around, close w/ sl st. Fasten off, weave in ends.
18	choice	With either color, work 4 rows in pattern. Close w sl st. Fasten off, weave in ends.

Flower
ch3, work 12 dc into 1st chain, close w/ sl st in top of 1st dc
ch1, in same st as sl st *sc, ch4, sc in next stitch; rep from * 6 times,
close w sl st in 1st ch. Fasten off, sew to hat, weave in ends.

**Work part B until hat measures x
inches from top**

Toddler 6
Youth   6.5
Adult   7

Finished length from top
(inches)
Toddler 7
Youth   7.5
Adult   8

My New Hooks

by Aimee Woolwine (aka AimeeCrochets)

When I first picked up a hook with the intention of using it, I was 25, a new mother, trying to figure out what was going on in my new world. My son's severe prematurity had prevented my return to a job I didn't think I wanted long-term anyway, but I had been earning nearly half our income before his birth. I can't remember why I began to crochet, maybe as a path to inexpensive gifting, but I made several afghans for baby and Christmas gifts, and I enjoyed myself.

On some level, I was surprised – not necessarily with the enjoyment, but with my satisfaction with the results. My previous experience with crochet was as the recipient of my grandmother's endeavors throughout my childhood. Brightly-colored pillow form covers, pom-pommed slippers I wore to elementary school over my swollen, bee-stung foot, several afghans (pronounced af-a-gans by Grandma), and a sweater sent to me in high school that had not benefitted from the words "sizing" or "shaping" or "style." I used them and wore them, loving the connection to a grandmother who lived thousands of miles away and cringing internally at the old-fashionedness of it all. Still, I never claimed to be fashionable, and I wore that sweater to high school, a hug from a woman an ocean and most of a continent away.

By the time my first son was born, Grandma had been gone for over five years. She had been my last surviving grandparent, and the only one who had met my husband, although she passed away a year before we were engaged. When I picked up that hook for the first time, I'd like to say I felt an instant connection across generations and time, but my life is not a novel. As a sleep deprived, post-partum despressioning mom of a high-needs preemie, my mind was simply on the hook and yarn and pattern, hopeful that the finished product would eventually match the picture on the skein wrapper or in the book, and, more than anything, thankful for the distraction. The more I hooked, though, the more tiny memories began niggling at the back of my brain until one day I felt the connection.

The connection – once I finally got it! – brought with it that warm, fuzzy feeling of contentment you'd expect. Still, as my son grew and his little brother joined the family, my hands became fuller, and the hooks and yarn were stashed away for "sometime soon." Now, years later, they've come back out with a vengeance, and my mother showed up with a gift for me last week: a collection of hand-turned wooden crochet hooks we had bought for Grandma during those high school years. Mom just happened to find them, and I just happen to be ready for them. I'm ready for the handiwork, and I'm ready for a renewal of that connection. And I'm ready to appreciate once again, at a deeper level, the love that went into those pom-poms, pillows and sweaters.

SCARLETT BLOSSOM

By Pyo (aka Pyogazel)

Who doesn't like flowers? Who hasn't dreamed of being ravishingly wrapped in a handful of them ? Well I least I have. Hence this sweater... It's the perfect addition to your wardrobe if you are not daring enough to wear a spaghetti or tube dress, and if you are... then the mesh fabric and lustful colours will certainly appeal to you !

~ Pyo

Materials:

Yarn : a shimmering sport or double knitting weight that knits up to 24 stitches for 4 inches (WPI : 12 or 13) in poppy red (MAIN COLOUR : about 400g) and deep lilac purple (CONTRASTING COLOUR : about 100 g).
Were used here :

Bouton d'or "Flash" (88% rayon 12% polyester ribbon yarn, 50g = 125m) in cerise (violet) 2 bobbins, and Lucifer (red) 8 bobbins.

Crochet hook : 3.5 mm
stitch marker,
contrasting colour satin ribbon (2 m)
contrasting colour 5mm beads (2)

GAUGE

5 flowers in a quincunx
= 19 stitches X 8 Rounds
= 9 X 9 cm unblocked
= 10 X 10 cm blocked

Size : S, M and L

Instructions are given for sizes (S) M (L)

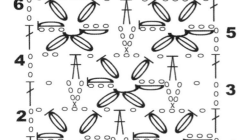

Special stitches:

Beginning petal :

→ Chain 3,
→ yarn over, insert hook in last chain 1 space of round below, yarn over and draw a loop, *yarn over and draw through one loop, yarn over and draw through two loops*, 2 loops on hook, repeat from * to * once, 3 loops on hook.

(beginning petal made)

Linking petal :

→ Chain 3,
→ yarn over, insert hook in third chain from hook, yarn over and draw a loop, *yarn over and draw through one loop, yarn over and draw through two loops* 2 loops on hook, repeat from * to * once, 3 loops on hook.

(linking petal made)

Incomplete petals set :

→ Chain 3,
→ yarn over, insert hook in last chain 1 space of round below, *yarn over, draw a loop, yarn over, pull through one loop, yarn over, pull through two loops on hook*, 2 loops on hook, repeat from * to * once, 3 loops on hook, pull through all loops on hook (first petal made),
→ chain 3, yarn over, insert hook on top of petal made, *yarn over, draw a loop, yarn over, pull through one loop, yarn over, pull through two loops on hook*, 2 loops on hook, repeat from * to * once, , 3 loops on hook, pull through all loops on hook (second petal made)

Petal :

→ yarn over, insert hook in stitch or space specified, yarn over and draw a loop, (yarn over and draw through one loop, yarn over and draw through two loops, 2 loops on hook, repeat from * to * twice, 4 loops on hook.

(petal made)

Incomplete petals set :

- → Chain 3,
- → yarn over, insert hook in last chain 1 space of round below, *yarn over, draw a loop, yarn over, pull through one loop, yarn over, pull through two loops on hook*, 2 loops on hook, repeat from * to * once, 3 loops on hook, pull through all loops on hook (first petal made),
- → chain 3, yarn over, insert hook on top of petal made, *yarn over, draw a loop, yarn over, pull through one loop, yarn over, pull through two loops on hook*, 2 loops on hook, repeat from * to * once, , 3 loops on hook, pull through all loops on hook (second petal made)
  (incomplete petals set made),

Petals set :

- → chain 3,
- → yarn over, insert hook in third chain from hook, *yarn over, draw a loop, yarn over, pull through one loop, yarn over, pull through two loops on hook*, repeat from * to * once, 3 loops on hook, (linking petal made),
- → yarn over, insert hook in following chain 1 space, *yarn over, draw a loop, yarn over, pull through one loop, yarn over, pull through two loops on hook*, repeat from * to * twice, 7 loops on hook (second petal made),
- → yarn over, insert hook in following chain 1 space, *yarn over, draw a loop, yarn over, pull through one loop, yarn over, pull through two loops on hook*, repeat from * to * twice, 11 loops on hook, (third petal made),
- → pull through all loops on hook, chain 3, yarn over, insert hook on top of the three petals made, *yarn over, draw a loop, yarn over, pull through one loop, yarn over, pull through two loops on hook*, repeat from * to * once, 3 loops on hook, pull through all loops on hook (fourth petal made)

(petals set made

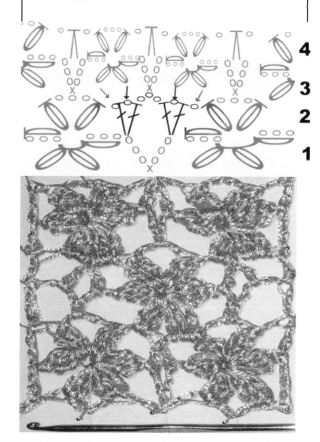

TIP :
Always pull tight when pulling through all loops on hook : the heart of the flowers will be tinier.

IN CONTRASTING COLOUR

Foundation Chain (184) 195 (206), slip stitch the circle closed

Round 1 Beginning petal in first foundation chain, 3 loops on hook, skip 4, petal in sixth foundation chain, 7
loops on hook, pull through all loops on hook, beginning petal on top of 2 petals made,
(first petals set made)
Skip 2, chain 3, single crochet in ninth foundation chain, chain 3, [linking petal, skip 2, petal in
following stitch, skip 4, petal in following stitch, 11 loops on hook, pull through all loops on hook, linking
petal on top of 3 petals made,
Skip 2, chain 3, single crochet in following stitch, chain 3]
Repeat from [to] (15) 16 (17) times, slip stitch and linking petal on top of first petals set made (last
petal of first set made)

Round 2 Beginning petal on top of first petals set made on round below, pull through all loops on hook (fifth petal made),
beginning petal on top of same petals set, pull through all loops on hook (sixth petal made),
(first flower complete)
chain 1, double crochet 2 together in the first chain before and third chain after following sc of round below, chain 1,
(cluster made)
[petal on top of the following petals set of round below, pull through all loops on hook (fifth petal made), chain 3, petal on
top of same petals set, pull through all loops on hook (sixth petal made),
(flower complete)
chain 1, double crochet 2 together in first chain before and third chain after following sc of round below, chain 1, (cluster
made)]
repeat from [to] around, **replace cluster at centre of round with an increase**, finish round with slip stitch in third chain
of beginning petal of the round.
(first row of flowers made)

Round 3 Incomplete petals set ,
chain 3, single crochet in following chain 3 space, chain 3, [petals set , chain 3, single crochet in following chain 3
space, chain 3]
Repeat from [to] around, linking petal, (third petal of first set made), petal in chain 1 space before last of round below, 7
loops on hook, pull through all loops on hook (last petal of first set made)
end with slip stitch on top of Incomplete petals set at beginning of round.

Round 4 Like Round 2
(second row of flowers made)

IN MAIN COLOUR

Round 5 Like Round 3

Round 6 Like Round 2
(third row of flowers made)

IN CONTRASTING COLOUR

Round 7   Like Round 3

Round 8   Like Round 2
(fourth row of flowers made)

IN MAIN COLOUR

Round 9   Like Round 3

Round 10   Like Round 2
(fifth row of flowers made)

Size S : start armholes and body

IN CONTRASTING COLOUR

Round 11   Like Round 3

Round 12   Like Round 2
(sixth row of flowers made)

Size M : start armholes and body

IN MAIN COLOUR

Round 13   Like Round 3

Round 14   Like Round 2
(seventh row of flowers made)

Size L : start armholes and body
Armholes and body :

IN MAIN COLOUR

Round 15   Size S, do this round IN CONTRASTING COLOUR
{ [Chain 4, yarn over, insert hook in third chain from hook,
*yarn over, draw a loop, yarn over, pull through one loop, yarn
over, pull through two loops on hook*, repeat from * to * once,
pull through all loops on hook (one underarm petal made)],
repeat from [to] (5) 7 (9) times,
skip 5 "flowers", (first armhole) [petals set , chain 3, single
crochet in following chain 3 space, chain 3], repeat from [to]
(5) 6 (6) times } (back), repeat from { to } (second armhole
and front)
slip stitch in first chain of round, chain 3, slip stitch in fourth
chain of round

Try the yoke out, see if the armholes feel comfortable although close fitting,
worn normally or upside down, make the necessary adjustments by adding
groups of 2 underarm petals to them

Round 16 Size S, do this round IN CONTRASTING COLOUR
Beginning petal in chain 1 space between 2 underarm petals, pull through all loops on hook, chain 3, petal in same stitch as previous one, pull through all loops on hook (flower complete)
chain 1, double crochet 2 together in following chain 1 space between 2 petals, chain 1 (cluster made)
{ [petal in following chain 1 space between 2 underarm petals, pull through all loops on hook, chain 3, petal in same stitch as previous one, pull through all loops on hook,
(flower complete)
chain 1, double crochet 2 together in following chain 1 space between 2 petals, chain 1 (cluster made)]
repeat from [to] throughout armhole,
[petal on top of the following petals set made on round below, pull through all loops on hook, chain 3, petal on top of same petals set, pull through all loops on hook),
(flower complete)
chain 1, double crochet 2 together in first chain before and third chain after following sc of round below, chain 1, (cluster made)], } repeat from [to] until you reach second armhole, then repeat from { to }

Round 17 Size S : this round and following IN MAIN COLOUR
Like Round 3

Round 18 Like Round 2, but without increases

Round 19 Like Round 3
Round 20 Like Round 2, but without increases
Round 21 Like Round 3

Round 22 Decrease:
Beginning petal on top of the first petals set made on round below, pull through all loops on hook,
chain 1, do not make petal, do not complete flower
chain 1 do not make cluster,
chain 1, petal on top of following petals, pull all loops on hook
chain 1, double crochet 2 together in first chain before and third chain after following sc of round below, chain 1, (cluster made) (decrease complete)
[petal on top of following petals set of round below, pull through all loops on hook, chain 3, petal on top of same petals set, pull through all loops on hook (flower complete)
chain 1, double crochet 2 together in first chain before and third chain after following sc of round below, chain 1, (cluster made)]
repeat from [to] until you reach second armhole, work another decrease, then repeat from [to] around, end with slip stitch in third chain of beginning petal of round.

Round 23	Like Round 3
Round 24	Like Round 2 but without increases
Round 25	Like round 3
Round 26	Like Round 2 but without increases
Round 27	Like round 3
Round 28	Like Round 22
Round 29	Like round 3
Round 30	Like Round 2 but without increases
Round 31	Like Round 3
Round 32	Like Round 22
Round 33	Like round 3

Round 34   Border :
* Beginning petal on top of the first petals set of round below, pull through all loops on hook, chain 3, slip stitch on top of same petals set *, chain 3, repeat from * to * (flower complete)
chain 3, single crochet in third chain before following sc of round below, work a picot, single crochet in third chain after following sc of round below, chain 3,
[slip stitch on top of following petals set of round below, * beginning petal on top of the first petals set of round below, pull through all loops on hook, chain 3, slip stitch on top of same petals set *, chain 3, repeat from * to * (flower complete) chain 3, single crochet in third chain before following sc of round below, work a picot, single crochet in third chain after following sc of round below, chain 3]
repeat from [to] around.

Finish off. Weave in ends. Start sleeves.

Sleeves :

r1:	Attach yarn at armhole, in a chain 1 space between two underarm petals of round 15, work like for Round 2 of the yoke, but without increases,
r2:	Like Round 3 of the yoke
r3 to r8 :	Like r1 and r2
r9:	work like for Round 2 of the yoke, but with one decrease worked at centre of round,
r10:	Like Round 3 of the yoke
r11 to 16:	Like r1 and r2

Finish off. Weave in ends.

Start collar.

Row 1:	Attach yarn at centre of front, beginning petal at centre of front, pull through all loops on hook, linking petal, skip 4, petal in following stitch, pull through all loops on hook, linking petal, pull through all loops on hook, skip 2, chain 3, single crochet in following stitch, chain 3 [linking petal, skip 2, petal in following stitch, skip 4, petal in following stitch, 11 loops on hook, pull through all loops on hook, linking petal on top of 3 petals made, pull through all loops on hook, skip 2, chain 3, single crochet in following stitch, chain 3] Repeat from [to] throughout, end with slip stitch on top of last petals set of row, turn
Row 2:	Beginning petal on top of last petals set of row below, pull through all loops on hook, chain 3, petal on top of same petals set, pull through all loops on hook (flower complete) [chain 1, double crochet 2 together in first chain before and third chain after following sc of row below, chain 1, (cluster made) petal on top of the following petals set, pull through all loops on hook, chain 3, petal on top of same petals set, pull through all loops on hook (flower complete)] repeat from [to] across, turn
Row 3	Chain 1, single crochet in last chain 3 space of row below, chain 3 [linking petal, petal in following chain 1 space, petal in following chain 1 space, 11 loops on hook, pull through all loops on hook, linking petal on top of 3 petals made, pull through all loops on hook, chain 3, single crochet in following chain 3 space, chain 3] Repeat from [to] across, chain 3, slip stitch on top of last petals set of row, turn
Row 4:	Like row 2
Row 5:	Like row 3
Row 6:	Border : Starting on top of last petals set of row below, work like Round 34 of the yoke Finish off. Weave in ends.

Weave a ribbon in the aperture of the collar and put one bead at each end of the ribbon
Wear...

Collar up tied closed

Collar up without a tie

Part II

Hookalicious

Since we in the CLF have a thing for dictionary definitions*, I created one for

Hookalicious!

Hookalicious; adjective (huh-k-ah-lih-sh-uhs): 1. Something divinely constructed utilizing the eminent fiber art medium known as crochet. 2. An item that is crocheted with paramount skill.

3. A crocheted garment or article that so defies conventional mythos surrounding crochet that it inspires awe: Vernacular slang: To express appreciation of a crocheted item, or a crochet enthusiasts skills, e.g.: "Yo! Dude that sweater is totally Hookalicious!" or "Whoa! That's one Hookalicious babe!"

Related: Hookilicious, similar definition and alternate spelling, depending on the whim of the Fearless Leader at time of writing blog posts.

*this refers to the time we flooded Merriam Webster Company with emails regarding an online definition of crochet that was inaccurate. It had nothing to do with Merriam Webster at all, and they were very sweet about the whole thing. It was still a cool start to action,that you can read about it on the blog.

It always amazes me that people say something can't be crocheted.

In my most unhumble opinion that means that they just didn't have a great deal of imagination...

Hookalicious

What does Hookalicious mean to me? Something that is delectable, an item that makes me gasp when I see the photo, or something a bit ground breaking, or even something simple that makes me say to myself, "Why didn't I think of doing that?"

In this section we have all manner of things to make you drool, or want to branch out beyond your normal crochet habits.

There is nothing wrong with making lots of hats, scarves, or afghans. Don't listen to the silly folks who say otherwise. Part of being a Hookalicious member of the CLF is understanding that YOU are one Hookalicious human.

Think of all the great things you have made for yourself or others. Think of the love that inspired them, or how things helped you cope.

I'm not a crafting snob; I think that the most important thing in any crafter's life is the fact that they use their creative powers. Using creative force to produce items that can, and often do, embody love and all the ways that love can be expressed.

Remember, many people come to our chosen craft through older relatives, or from being inspired by a memory of a bye gone day. Read the articles in this section, they are bound to make you laugh, and some will make you tear up. For we, who dub ourselves crocheters, know just how important our little bent stick and some yarn can be...or do we? If you don't right now, hopefully you will by the end of this section.

Hook on, Live Long My friends!!!

Laurie Wheeler

Crochet Cabled Fingerless Gloves

By Jennifer Reeve (aka CraftKitten)

Photo and pattern © 2008 Jennifer Reeve

Editor's note: And they say we can't make cables! Of course you can crochet cables. It just takes a little practice to make them nice and polished! As with any craft, the more advanced stitches take a bit of getting used to making, why not practice on these beautiful gloves!

This pattern is more advanced.

Materials:

Materials: approximately 200 yards fingering weight yarn.

(I suggest using a solid color or if you use a variegated yarn one that isn't too busy so that you can see the cables.)

Size D 3.25 mm hook.

3 locking stitch markers.

Special Stitch Instructions, US terms

Cable Cross:

Skipping 2 Fpdc, work Fptr around each of next 2 Fpdc, then skip back to the 2 hdc in the middle and work 1 hdc in each hdc, then crossing back to the first 2 Fpdc skipped, work 1 Fptr in each fpdc.

Fpdc = Front Post Double Crochet

Fptr= Front Post Treble Crochet

Right Glove	
Base Chain	Ch 44, join with slst to form ring.
Rnd 1	Ch 3, 1 dc in each chain around, join with slst to top of ch 3. Turn.
Rnd 2	: Ch 2, 1 hdc in next st, Bpdc around each of the next 2 sts,[hdc in each of next 2 sts, Bpdc around the next 2 sts] repeat around. Join with slst to top of ch 2. Turn.
Rnd 3	Ch 2 *[Fpdc around each of the next 2 sts, hdc in each of the next 2 sts]** 4 times, [Cable Cross] 2 times, hdc in each of next 2 hdc, rep from * to ** around ending with 2 hdc, join with slst to top of ch 2. Turn.
Rnd 4	Ch 2, 1 hdc in next st, Bpdc around each of the next 2 sts,[hdc in each of next 2 sts, Bpdc around the next 2 sts] repeat around. Join with slst to top of ch 2. Turn.
Rnd 5	Ch 2 [Fpdc around each of the next 2 sts, hdc in each of the next 2 sts] rep around, join with slst to top of ch 2.
Rnd 6	Ch 2, 1 hdc in next st, Bpdc around each of the next 2 sts,[hdc in each of next 2 sts, Bpdc around the next 2 sts] repeat around. Join with slst to top of ch 2. Turn
Rnd 7	Rep rnd 3-6 twice, **then rnd 3 once more.**
Rnd 16	:Ch 2, hdc in each of the next 7 sts, 2hdc in each of next 2sts, [Bpdc around each of the next 2 sts, hdc in each of next 2 sts] 6 times, hdc in each st around, join with slst to top of ch 2. Turn.
Rnd 17	Ch 2, hdc in each of next 12 sts [Fpdc around each of the next 2 sts, hdc in each of the next 2 sts] 5 times, 2 hdc in each of the next 2 sts, hdc in each st around, join with slst to top of ch2. Turn.

Right Glove Continued	
Rnd 18-27	Work even in established pattern.
Rnd:28	Ch 2, hdc in each of the next 11 sts, 2 hdc in each of next 2sts, [Bpdc around each of the next 2 sts, hdc in each of next 2 sts] 6 times, hdc in each st around, join with slst to top of ch 2. Turn.
Rnd: 29-30	Rnd 29 & 30: Work even in established pattern.
Thumb Hole: Do Not Turn! Ch 12, join to hdc just before the Bpdc (before Rib). Turn.	
Rnd: 31	Ch 2, hdc in each ch and then in each hdc, Fpdc around each of the next 2 sts, hdc in each of the next 2 sts, Cable Cross, Fpdc around each of the next 2 sts, hdc in each of the next 2 sts, hdc in each st around, join with slst to top of ch2. Turn
Rnd 32-39	work even in established pattern. Fasten off.

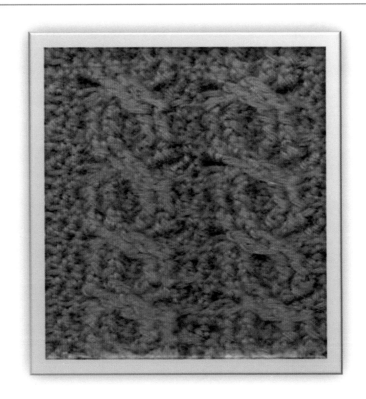

Left Glove	
Base Chain	Ch 44, join with sl st to form ring.
Rnd 1	Ch 3, 1 dc in each chain around, join with slst to top of ch 3. Turn.
Rnd 2	Ch 2, 1 hdc in next st, Bpdc around each of the next 2 sts,[hdc in each of next 2 sts, Bpdc around the next 2 sts] repeat around. Join with slst to top of ch 2. Turn
Rnd 3	Ch 2 *[Fpdc around each of the next 2 sts, hdc in each of the next 2 sts]** 3 times, [Cable Cross] 2 times, hdc in each of next 2 hdc, rep from * to ** around ending with 2 hdc, join with slst to top of ch 2. Turn.
Rnd 4	Ch 2, 1 hdc in next st, Bpdc around each of the next 2 sts,[hdc in each of next 2 sts, Bpdc around the next 2 sts] repeat around. Join with slst to top of ch 2. Turn.

Rnd 5	Ch 2 [Fpdc around each of the next 2 sts, hdc in each of the next 2 sts] rep around, join with slst to top of ch 2.
Rnd 6`	Ch 2, 1 hdc in next st, Bpdc around each of the next 2 sts,[hdc in each of next 2 sts, Bpdc around the next 2 sts] repeat around. Join with slst to top of ch 2. Turn
Rnd 5-15	**Repeat rnds 3-6 twice, then rnd 3 once more**

Rnd. 16	**Ch 2, hdc in each of the next 13 sts [Bpdc around each of the next 2 sts, hdc in each of next 2 sts] 6 times, 2hdc in each of next 2sts, hdc in each st around, join with slst to top of ch 2. Turn.**
Rnd 17	Ch 2, hdc in each of next 8 sts, 2 hdc in each of the next 2 sts, [Fpdc around each of the next 2 sts, hdc in each of the next 2 sts] 5 times, hdc in each st around, join with slst to top of ch2. Turn.
Rnd 18-27	Work even in established pattern.
Rnd 28	Ch 2, hdc in each of the next 11 sts, 2 hdc in each of next 2sts, [Bpdc around each of the next 2 sts, hdc in each of next 2 sts] 6 times, hdc in each st around, join with slst to top of ch 2. Turn.
Rnd 29 & 30	Work even in established pattern
Thumb Hole: (For this hand turn as normal) Ch 12, join to hdc just before the Bpdc. Turn.	
Rnd 31	Rnd 31: Ch 2, Fpdc around each of the next 2 sts, hdc in each of the next 2 sts, Cable Cross, Fpdc around each of the next 2 sts, hdc in each of the next 2 sts, hdc in each st and ch around, join with slst to top of ch2. Turn.
Rnd 32-39	work even in established pattern. Fasten off.
Thumb same for both hands)	Join with slst to corner on the top side of the mitt.
Rnd 1	Ch 2, hdc in each st, work hdc2tog twice at palm side corner, hdc in each st around. Join with slst to top of ch 2.
Rnd 2-4	Ch 2, hdc in each st, work hdc2tog once at palm side corner, hdc in each st around. Join with slst to top of ch 2. Fasten off.

Finger Holes

Note: You will be working in hdc snaking around each of your fingers and then back.

Put on gloves. Using locking stitch markers, pin gloves together between your fingers.	Left hand: On palm side of glove join with slst to st just to the left of the marker between your pointer and middle finger.
Rnd 1-Pointer Finger: Ch 2, hdc in each st around pointer finger to marker.	Right hand: On back side of glove join with slst to st just to the left of the marker between your pointer and middle finger.
Rnd 1-Middle Finger-Palm side: (replace marker to middle st) Skip to opposite side, hdc in each st to next marker.	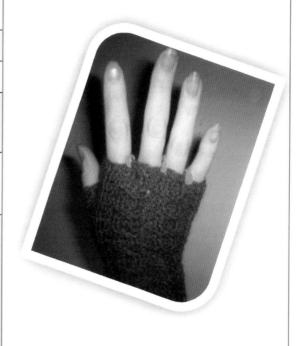
Rnd 1-Ring Finger-Back side: Skip to opposite side, hdc in each st to next marker.	
Rnd 1-Pinky Finger: Skip to opposite side, hdc in each st around pinky to marker.	
Rnd 1-Ring Finger-Palm side: Skip to opposite side, hdc in each st to next marker.	
Rnd 1-Middle Finger-Back side: Skip to opposite side, hdc in each st to next marker.	
Join with slst to top of Ch 2. Rnd 2- Ch 2 hdc in each st around each finger following "snake". Join with slst to top of ch 2.	

My father and I were both in our early twenties when we invited skulls into our lives. He was a sailor and I was a Peace Corps volunteer in highland Guatemala. He wore his to his grave, but mine is still in Guatemala.

Being an avid spelunker, I explored the caves around Jacaltenago where the pre-Columbian Maya elite were buried. The pottery had been taken earlier, but having no market value, the bones and skulls remained. I took one of the skulls with a flattened forehead, (signifying high rank(to town and placed it in my motorcycle helmet-shocking for some to see the empty eye sockets staring out at them, but it felt right to me. I also included it in a still life,(the only painting I did in Guatemala). The skull was with me when I moved to Xela a few years later, but it didn't accompany me to the United States. I couldn't return the skull to the cave, so I buried it on a scared mountain on the outskirts of the city. Later learning that it would have been illegal to export, I'm glad I listened to my inner voice. Years later I saw skulls and crossbones carved on the surfaces of many pre-Columbian Mayan ruins in the Yucatan. An archaeologist told me that they probably inspired the skull and crossbones motif of the early pirates of the Caribbean who frequented the area. Makes sense to me!

Prelude to the Tapestry Crochet UFO Bag

By Carol Ventura *(aka Tapestrycrochet)*
© 2008 Carol Ventura

Photo courtesy of Carol Ventura

A relief from a Mayan temple wall. Though to be the inspiration for the skull and cross bones flag of the

One of my father's tattoos was a skull earring and old fashioned sailor's hat. He was career Navy, and like his shipmatess, had a Navy inspired tattoo on each forearm. Analyzing my skull connection-I realize that it probably goes back to my dad. Growing up-associating skull is with him-made me put the skull in my helmet. That's why it comforted me when I was so far away from home instead of freaking me out! For medieval people and pirates, the skull represented death. For me, it brings back memories of my father and some of my adventures.

Now for some of the symbolism of this project:

One X handle for 4 skulls = all for one and one for all =

All 4 + 1 and 1 + 4 all = 10 = Roman numeral X.

Deep don't you think? Yes, this bag is a little over a foot deep-

A foot in the grave?

It's that darn corny gene showing it's head(s) again-you can blame my father for that, too.

Editor's note: When I got this submission in the mail, I laughed so hard! Since I'm a HUGE fan of all that's piratical this just had to have a home in the CLF First Ever Book!

Difficulty: Advanced or for the Very Patient!

(Here you go folks; you wanted something to sink your teeth into! How about this FUNKY project!

Materials:

Hook: Steel crochet hook size 00 (or size that will make appropriate gauge)

4 spools ea (200 g/180m) black (color 19) and 2 spools of ivory (color #3) size 18 Omega La Espiga Nylon thread.

Stitch Marker

Gauge: 25 stitches and 19 rows = 4inches.

Size: 11' Diameter by 12/12" high (without handles)

Abbreviations:

ch=chain   rnd=round

inc=increase   sc=single crochet

lp(s)=loops   sl st=slip stitch

rem=remain   st(s)=stitch(es)

Tapestry UFO Bag Pattern by Carol Ventura

© 2008 Carol Ventura

Before you start here are some tips:

This piece is worked as a spiral, so DO NOT JOIN. To keep track of where each round (rnd) ends, slip a stitch (st) marker into the top of the last stitch of the round and then remove it and place it in the last stitch of each round.

Special Stitches

To carry other color: Lay other color over top of stitches being worked into, then single crochet across as usual, encasing it between stitches. If done correctly, it will not be visible from front or back of work.

To Change color in tapestry crochet:

Work stitch until w loops remain on hook, drop working color, pick up non-working (carried) color and draw through both loops on hook.

Starting at center, ch 4 with black, leaving 6" tail at beginning of ch; join with sl st to form a ring.	
Rnd 1: Sc 6 into the ring (while carrying tail)	Rnd 16: Inc. every tenth stitch. (132)
Rnd 2:Continue to carry tail. Inc by crocheting 2 sts into each st. (12)	Rnd 17: Inc in every eleventh st. (144)
Rnd 3: Inc. every stitch. (24)	Rnd 18: Crochet into each stitch (no increases) (144)
Rnd 4: Cut tail and begin carrying bone. Inc in every second st. (36)	Rnd 19: Inc in every twelfth stitch (156)
Rnd 5: sc into each stitch (no increases) (36)	Rnd 20: Inc in every thirteenth stitch. (168)
Rnd 6: Inc in every third st. (48)	Rnd 21: Crochet into each stitch (no increases) (168)
Rnd 7: Inc in every fourth st. (60)	Rnd 22: Inc in every fourteenth stitch (180)
Rnd 8: Inc in every fifth st. (72)	Rnd 23: Inc in every fifteenth stitch (192)
Rnd 9: Crochet into each stitch. (no increases) (72)	Rnd 24: Crochet into each stitch (no increases) (192)
Rnd 10: Inc in every sixth stitch (84)	Rnd 25: Inc in every sixteenth stitch (204)
Rnd 11: Inc in every seventh stitch. (96)	
Rnd 12: Crochet into ea h stitch (no increases) (96)	
Rnd 13: Inc in every eighth stitch. (108)	
Rnd 14: Inc in every ninth st. (120)	
Rnd 15: Crochet into ea st (no increases) (120)	

Rnd A: Remove st. marker, sc 4 black, * sc 4 ivory, sc 2 black, sc 4 ivory, sc 41 black. Repeat from * four times.	**Rnd E: Sc 1 black, ^5 ivory, cut off black, ch 150 ivory, inset hook into 102snd stitch and began to carry black, sc 4 ivory, 42 black* Repeat from *-* 2 times. *Sc 4 Ivory, decrease 1 ivory, sc 148 ivory onto chain, decrease 1 ivory, tapestry crochet 3 ivory, 42 black*. Repeat from *-* 2 times.**
Rnd B: *sc 5 ivory, 1 black, 5 Ivory, 40 black. Repeat from* four times.	**RndF:** Sc ``1 black, *sc 3 ivory, decrease 1 ivory, sc 148(onto the bottom of the chain), decrease 1 ivory, tapestry crochet 2 ivory, 43 black* repeat from *-* 2 times.
Rnd C: *sc 11 Ivory, 40 black.* Repeat from * four times.	**Rnd G**: Sc 1 black, *sc 2 ivory, decrease 1 ivory, sc 146 ivory ,decrease 1 Ivory, sc 2 ivory,44 black*. Repeat from*-* 2 times.*Sc 2Ivory, decrease 1 ivory, sc 146 Ivory onto chain, decrease 1ivory, tapestry crochet 1 ivory, sc 44 black*> Repeat from *-* 2 times.
Rnd D: Sc 1 black,*10 ivory, 41 black. Repeat from * four times.	**Rnd H:** Sc 1 black, sc 1 ivory, decrease 1 ivory, sc 146 ivory,decrease 1 ivory, sc 1 ivory, sc 45 black, sc 1 ivory, decrese 1 ivory, sc 146 ivory, cut the black, decrease 1 ivory, sl st 1 ivory, cut the ivory (leaving an 8 inch tail). Pull the tail through the loop, work the tail back and forth up the top loops of the strap for 4 inches to secure it, the cut off remaining tail.

Now you have somewhere to put you UnFinished Objects – but please don't make it their final resting place! Hopefully, you'll be inspired to resurrect and finish them someday soon!

Follow the graph for rnds 26-80, <u>repeating the motif four times for each rnd.</u>
(Editor's note: Repeating the motif four times, means there will be four skull and cross bones represented on the bag.)

The graph is for right handed crocheters, left handed crocheters should look at the reversed image of the graph in a mirror.

About the Author:

Dr. Carol Ventura teaches art history at Tennessee Technological University. Her interest in Tapestry Crochet was sparked in the 1970's by colorful Guatemalan tapestry crocheted shoulder bags. Since that time she's explored the design potential of the technique, developed a system of diagramming patterns, and created a variety of flat and three dimensional projects, which she shares in her tapestry crochet books and videos. For more information please look at her website: www.tapestrycrochet.com

You Got Math In My Crochet

(Or On the Grid) –

Using Spreadsheet Programs to do Designing Calculations
By Shevon Retske (Fibernerd)

When you think "spreadsheet" or "math", crochet is probably not the first thing that comes to mind. It's understandable, because it's common belief that you're either creative or technical, but not both at the same time. This just isn't true.

I'm one of those "math people" who's also a "creative person". I think of math as a set of tools that can help us better understand the world around us, crochet included. Just a little bit of "design math" goes a long way to making it easier to make your crochet do what you want it to, releasing you from the binds of patterns. Of course, you can also experiment (improvise) and try what works without planning, but understanding some simple relationships will even make that easier. And I promise I'll try not to put you to sleep.

WHY SPREADSHEETS?

Spreadsheet programs are a part of my everyday life. I've used them for everything from school and work assignments, calculate a car loan, balance my checkbook, and all sorts of fun and interesting things. They're also useful for creating and modifying patterns.

Why would someone want to go through the hassle of using a whole spreadsheet to do a few calculations?
- They're very easy to use for the basics.
- It's easier to see how things are calculated and harder to make a mistake.
- You can change things without having to redo all of your work.
- They're neat and easy to read.
- You can distribute them easily.

THE FUN PART: THE MATH

If there's one thing you take away from this article, I hope it's this: You can solve most problems in crochet by reasoning it out. Use whichever way comes naturally to you. Since it's I'm a visual thinker, and crocheted objects are tangible and often 2 dimensional, I usually think it out by drawing pictures, in my mind, on scrap paper or in a spreadsheet. I just think it out, and I try to find a way to check back.

For a simple example, let's figure out how to get gauge. Assume I'm making a sweater. Since I'm a good little crocheter and I always crochet a generous swatch and wash it as I intend to wash the finished product, (This is purely hypothetical and would almost never happen in reality). The recommended gauge is 12 stitches over 4 inches (or 12/4 = 3 stitches per inch) in pattern, on a size J (6 mm) hook. When I do my swatch and wash it, with the recommended hook size, I come out with a gauge of about 16 stitches over 4 inches (or 16/4 = 4 stitches per inch). Do I need to go up or down in hook size?

If I'm getting 16 stitches over 4 inches, I have more stitches in one inch than I'm supposed to, so my stitches are too small. Thus I need a larger hook to get larger stitches.

Here's how I would draw this example out.

Here are the basic relationships for flat shapes:

- width = (number of stitches) x (stitches per inch)
- length = (number of rows) x (rows per inch)

SPREADSHEET BASICS

There are several spreadsheet programs that you can use. Microsoft Excel is one of the most popular ones, and is included in the Microsoft Office suite of programs. OpenOffice is a suite of programs comparable to Microsoft Office, that is available for free at www.openoffice.org. The Calc program there is very intuitive and easy to use. Google Docs, also free, is a web based application. Your spreadsheets are saved online, not on your computer, and can be easily shared. Any of these would be easy for a beginner to learn.

Once you open your spreadsheet, you will notice a few things. The most basic unit is called a cell. It is a small box that can have either text or a formula input. Cells are arranged in vertical columns (designated by letters) and horizontal rows (designated by numbers). The arrangement of cells and columns is called a worksheet. A workbook (or spreadsheet file) can have multiple worksheets. Tabs at the bottom of the screen allow you to switch between worksheets.

You can input either text or formulas into each cell. For instance I can type SC per Inch in a cell, or type =20/4. After typing a formula in a cell, the results of the formula are displayed in the cell (in the second example above, the cell displays 5).

In order to display text and do calculations in one cell, enclose the text in quotes, and separate the formulas and text with ampersands (&). For example, in one cell I could type = 20/4 & " stitches per " & 1 & " inch." which would display 5 stitches per 1 inch. Make sure that you add spaces and punctuation inside the quotes.

Here are some examples:

	A	B	C	
1				
2		SC Per Inch	5	
3				
4		5 SC Per 1 Inch		
5				
6		5 SC Per Inch		

The functions that you will need are the same ones on the simplest calculators: addition, subtraction, multiplication and division. You can do all sorts of crazy and complicated things with spreadsheets, but this is all you really need.

When working with these sheets, I like to use different colors for the numbers that are inputs than those that are calculated by formulas. This makes it easier to tell what numbers to change and which ones to leave alone. I keep values that I've entered in blue, and formulas in black.

For more detailed information, see the Help guide on your particular program.

CREATING A PATTERN

When creating a pattern, I find it's best to have one worksheet with all the numbers and calculations (called "Inputs"), and another with the instructions written out (called "Pattern").

For example, the general rule of thumb for creating a flat circle is to increase in each row the same number of stitches as in the first round. So, if you start with 5 stitches, increase 5 stitches each row, you'll increase 5 stitches.

To create a pattern for this, flat circle over 5 rounds, I would create a new workbook, with "Inputs" and "Pattern" worksheets.

The inputs page would have one input cell with the original number of stitches, and one formula cell for the number of stitches in each additional row

	A	B	C	D
1				
2		Increase per Row	5	
3				
4		Row 1	=C2	
5				
6		Row 2	=C4+C2	
7				
8		Row 3	=C6+C2	
9				
10				
11				

Formulas

	A	B	C
1			
2		Increase per Row	5
3			
4		Row 1	5
5			
6		Row 2	10
7			
8		Row 3	15
9			

Results

Formulaa

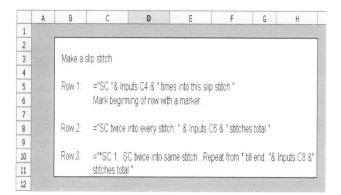

Results

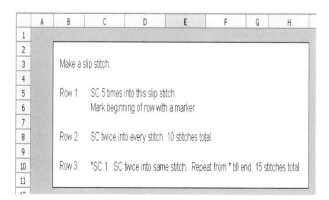

I've done a little bit of formatting with the Pattern page. The biggest difference is that the grid lines are turned off. These are what make a spreadsheet look like a spreadsheet.

It is easy to make modifications to the calculations in the spreadsheet. To change this pattern to start with 6 stitches, just change the "Increases per Row" cell on the Inputs sheet. The Pattern page would have updated numbers but look the same. To start with a different number of stitches than your increases per row, just type over the formula in the "Row 1" cell on the Inputs sheet.

As you can see, spreadsheets can produce some very professional looking documents with little work.

Yarn :
⇨150 g sport weight rayon with a Wrap per Inch of 13 in aqua blue (MAIN COLOUR)

(here: Cabotine by Bouton d'or in 'aqua', 90% rayon, 10 % cotton, 50g=87m, crochets up to 22 st for 4" with US 4 hooks)

⇨50 g of sport weight cotton with a Wrap per Inch of 12 in white (CONTRASTING COLOUR)

(here: Louxor by Anny Blatt in 'blanc', 100 % cotton, 50g=140m, knits up to 25 st for 4" with US 4 hooks)

Crochet hooks :
4 mm conventional crochet hook
6 mm Tunisian crochet hook
Yarn needle

ONDINE

By Pyo (Pyogazel)

"Tunisian crochet is a very versatile and fun technique. Some say it's like knitting with one needle.
I like it because it's quick and results in a fabric that is even and drapes well.
This top uses both conventional and Tunisian crochet, it is worked sideways with short rows to provide a flattering hourglass figure and a slimming texture.
As you will be constructing a rectangle from side to side, bear in mind that the right border of your project is in fact the bottom edge of the finished garment. "

Size show: Large. (Pattern for small, med, and large)

GAUGE

Tunisian swatch gauge :

Chain 13, alternate 4 rows of Tunisian knit stitch and 1 row of Tunisian double crochet.

10 rows X 13 stitches = 10 X 10 cm

Crochet seed stitch swatch gauge :

18 rows X 16 stitches = 10 X 10 cm

V stitch swatch gauge :

6 rows X 16 stitches = 10 X 10cm.

Tunisian knit stitch :

→ Chain 13,

→ Yarn over, insert your hook in the hump of the first stitch from hook, draw a loop, keep the loop on hook, *yarn over, insert your hook in the hump of following stitch, draw a loop, keep the loop on hook *, repeat from * to * across, do not turn,
to complete the row yarn over, pull through one loop on the hook, *yarn over, pull through two loops on the hook*, repeat from * to * across, do not turn,

→ *Yarn over, insert your hook in the middle of the loop from row below (between the two vertical bars far form a loop), draw a loop, keep the loop on hook*, repeat from * to * across, do not turn,
to complete the row yarn over, pull through one loop on the hook, *yarn over, pull through two loops on the hook*, repeat from * to * across, do not turn,

Tunisian double crochet :

→ Chain 15,

→ Yarn over, insert your hook in the hump of the third stitch from hook, draw a loop, yarn over, pull through one loop, yarn over, pull through two loops on the hook, *yarn over, insert your hook in the hump of following stitch, draw a loop, yarn over, pull through one loop, yarn over, pull through two loops on the hook *, repeat from * to * across, do not turn,
to complete the row yarn over, pull through one loop on the hook, *yarn over, pull through two loops on the hook*, repeat from * to * across

→ *yarn over, insert your hook in following stitch, draw a loop, yarn over, pull through one loop, yarn over, pull through two loops on the hook*, repeat from * to * across, do not turn,
to complete the row yarn over, pull through one loop on the hook, *yarn over, pull through two loops on the hook*, repeat from * to * across

Front post double crochet : (used on ruffle)

→ Reaching from front to back and front again, grab the yarn moving your hook from right to left around the post of the stitch from row below,

→ Yarn over, draw 1 loop

→ Yarn over, draw through 1 loop on the hook,

→ Yarn over, draw through 2 loops on the hook

→ Yarn over, draw through the 2 loops on the hook.

BODY: **With Tunisian hook, in aqua (MAIN COLOUR) only**

Foundation: **Chain 30**
Row 1: Back
Pull up a loop from each chain across, do not turn, complete the row : yarn over, pull through one loop on the hook, *yarn over, pull through two loops on the hook*, repeat from * to * across, do not turn, (30 Tunisian simple stitches),

Row 2: Inserting your hook between the two vertical bars, pull up a loop from each stitch across, do not turn, complete the row (30 Tunisian knit stitches),
Row 3 & 4: Like row 2

Row 5: Chain 2 (counts for 1 double crochet), *yarn over, inserting your hook between the two vertical bars, draw a loop, yarn over, pull through one loop, yarn over, pull through two loops on the hook*, repeat from * to * across, do not turn, complete the row , (30 Tunisian double crochet stitches),

Row 6 to 9   Like row 2

Row 10   Like row 5

Row 11 to 14   Like row 2

Row 15   Like row 5

<u>**Size L:**</u> Repeat Rows 11-15

Row 16 to 19   Like row 2

Row 20   Like row 5

Row 21 to 24   **Like row 2**

Row 25
Beginning armhole
Chain 1, yarn over, draw a loop, yarn over, pull through two loops on the hook*, repeat from * to*
again three times, yarn over, pull through all the loops on the hook (one cluster made) *yarn over, inserting your hook between the two vertical bars, draw a loop, yarn over, pull through one loop, yarn over, pull through two loops on the hook*, repeat from * to * across, do not turn, complete the row , (1 cluster and 26 Tunisian double crochet stitches),

Row 36 and following : Front

Size S : repeat rows 2 to 10 once, 11 to 15 twice, then 16 to 35 once,
 finish off,
sew bottom of row 1 (back) to top of repeat of row 35 (2nd

Row 26 **Inserting your hook between the two vertical bars, pull up a loop from 16 stitches, do not turn, complete the row (16 Tunisian knit stitches),**

Row 27   Inserting your hook between the two vertical bars, pull up a loop from all stitches from row below and remaining 10 stitches from two rows below, do not turn, complete the row (26

	Tunisian knit stitches),	armhole) and start the ruffle
Row 28	Like row 26	Size M repeat rows 2 to 24 twice, then 25 to 35 once,
Row 29	Like row 27	finish off,
Row 30	Like row 5 (26 Tunisian double crochet stitches)	sew bottom of row 1 (back) to top of repeat of row 35 (2nd armhole)
Row 31 to 34	Like rows 26 to 29	and start the ruffle
Row 35	Finishing armhole Chain 2 (counts for 1 double crochet), *yarn over, inserting your hook between the two vertical bars of the first stitch from row below, draw a loop, yarn over, pull through one loop, yarn over, pull through two loops on the hook*, repeat from * to * again three times, *yarn over, inserting your hook between the two vertical bars of following stitch, draw a loop, yarn over, pull through one loop, yarn over pull through two loops on the hook*, repeat from * to * across, do not turn, complete the row , (1 fan and 26 Tunisian double crochet stitches),	Size L repeat rows 2 to 16 three times, 17 to 24 once, then 25 to 35 finish off, sew bottom of row 1 (back) to top of repeat of row 35 (2nd armhole) and start the ruffle

RUFFLE:

With 4mm hook

Round 1: In white (CONTRASTING COLOUR) :
Working on the bottom edge of the garment, attach yarn to the short row rib on the wrong side of the garment, chain 3, 2 front post double crochet around the same, chain 2, 1 front post double crochet around the following short row rib bottom stitch, 1 double crochet, 1 front post double crochet around the following short row rib stitch, chain 2, *1 front post double crochet around the bottom stitch of the following 3 ribs, chain 2*, repeat from * to * then, reaching the second short rows part of the garment, 3 front post double crochet around the stitch at the bottom of the rib, chain 2, 1 front post double crochet around the following short row rib bottom stitch, 1 double crochet, 1 front post double crochet around the following short row rib stitch, chain 2, *1 front post double crochet around the bottom stitch of the following 3 ribs, chain 2*, repeat from * to *, finish round with a slip stitch in third chain of round.

Round 2: Chain 4, 1 double crochet on top of front post double crochet from round below, chain 1, skip 1 front post double crochet, 1 double crochet on top of following (third) front post double crochet, chain 1, 1 double crochet on top of same (third) front post double crochet (V stitch made) *chain 2, 1 double crochet on top of following front post double crochet from round below, chain 1, 1 double crochet on top of same front post double crochet, chain 1, skip 1 front post double crochet, 1 double crochet on top of following front post double crochet, chain 1, 1 double crochet on top of same front post double crochet *, repeat from * to *, finish round with a slip stitch in third chain of round.

Round 3 : Slip stitch in chain 1 space, chain 4, 1 double crochet in same chain 1 space, chain 1, [1 double crochet, chain 1, 1 double crochet] in chain 1 space from the following V stitch, *chain 2, [1 double crochet, chain 1, 1 double crochet] in chain 1 space from the following V stitch, chain 1, [1 double crochet, chain 1, 1 double crochet] in chain 1 space from the following V stitch *, repeat from * to * , finish round with a slip stitch in third chain of round

Round 4: Like round 3

Round 5: Slip stitch in chain 1 space, chain 4, 1 double crochet in same chain 1 space, chain 2, [1 double crochet, chain 1, 1 double crochet] in chain 1 space from the following V stitch, *chain 2, [1 double crochet, chain 1, 1 double crochet] in chain 1 space from the following V stitch, chain 2, [1 double crochet, chain 1, 1 double crochet] in chain 1 space from the following V stitch *, repeat from * to * , finish round with a slip stitch in third chain of round

Round 6: Slip stitch in chain 1 space, chain 4, 1 double crochet in same chain 1 space, chain 3, [1 double crochet, chain 1, 1 double crochet] in chain 1 space from the following V stitch, *chain 3, [1 double crochet, chain 1, 1 double crochet] in chain 1 space from the following V stitch, chain 3, [1 double crochet, chain 1, 1 double crochet] in chain 1 space from the following V stitch *, repeat from * to * , finish round with a slip stitch in third chain of round

Round 7   Like round 6, finish round with a slip stitch in third chain of round in aqua (MAIN COLOUR), don't cut white (CONTRASTING COLOUR) yarn

Round 8:   In aqua (MAIN COLOUR) :
One single crochet in third chain from round below, crochet one round in seed stitch, finish round with a slip stitch in first single crochet of round in white (CONTRASTING COLOUR), cut aqua (MAIN COLOUR) yarn

Round 9:   In white (CONTRASTING COLOUR) :
Chain 1, single crochet in following chain 1 space from round below, crochet one round in seed stitch, finish round with a slip stitch in first chain of round, cut white (CONTRASTING COLOUR) yarn.

Finish off, weave in ends, start borders and straps.

Special Stitch :

Crochet seed stitch :

Basically you single crochet in every chain space, and chain 1 to skip every single crochet from row below

row 0.   Chain 17,

row 1.   Sc in second chain from hook, *chain 1, skip 1 stitch from row below, single crochet in following stitch*, repeat from * to *, single crochet in last stitch from row below turn,

row 2.   chain 1, 1 single crochet, , *chain 1, skip 1 stitch from row below, single crochet in following stitch*, repeat from * to *, single crochet in last stitch from row below turn

repeat rows 1 and 2.

Front border, corner, wrong side

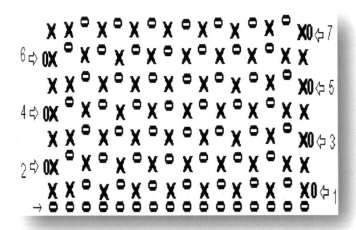

Row 1	In aqua (MAIN COLOUR) : Working on top of front border, attach yarn to one corner, chain 45, slip stitch in matching corner of back border, slip stitch in following stitch, turn
Row 2	crochet 1 row in seed stitch, turn
Row 3	In aqua (MAIN COLOUR) Like row 2
Row 4	In white (CONTRASTING COLOUR) Like row 2. Finish off.

Front border

Row 1	In white (CONTRASTING COLOUR) : Working on the upper edge of the garment, in the front, attach yarn to the top of the armhole (row 35), single crochet across the front until you reach top of second armhole
Row 2 to 4	Chain 1, crochet 1 row in seed stitch, turn
Row 5	In aqua (MAIN COLOUR) Like row 2
Row 6	In white (CONTRASTING COLOUR) Like row 2. Finish off.

Straps (check strap length and adjust to your liking before making the second one)

Row 1	In aqua (MAIN COLOUR) : Working on top of front border, attach yarn to one corner, chain 45 (or more if required), slip stitch in matching corner of back border, slip stitch in following stitch, turn
Row 2	crochet 1 row in seed stitch, one slip stitch in stitch following Row 1 on top of front border, finish with one slip stitch in following stitch, turn
Row 3	crochet 1 row in seed stitch, one slip stitch in stitch following Row 2 on top of back border finish with one slip stitch in following stitch, turn
Row 4	In white (CONTRASTING COLOUR) crochet 1 row in seed stitch, one slip stitch in stitch following Row 3 on top of front border, finish with one slip stitch in following stitch, turn
Row 5	In aqua (MAIN COLOUR) crochet 1 row in seed stitch, one slip stitch in stitch following Row 4 on top of back border, finish off, work second strap on top of the over corner of front border, working the same way as for strap 1 in aqua (MAIN COLOUR) only.

Finish off. Weave in ends. Wear.

Sticks and Strings and Other Things

By Shirley MacDonald
(cherryred on Ravelry)

I don't remember how old I was when my Mum taught me to crochet but I'm pretty sure it was well before I hit double figures. What I do know is that in primary seven, when all the other kids were busy knitting squares for charity blankets I turned up in class with my very own hook and insisted that I get to crochet with mine. My arguement that crochet was faster and nicer to look at than knit fabric must have struck a chord with the teacher since she just handed me a ball of yarn and let me get on with it. Maybe she was just glad that here was one small person who wouldn't be running to her in tears over dropped stitches.

After a few years of granny squares that never got sewn together and rather shapeless Barbie dresses my interest waned and eventually I stopped crocheting altogether. There were other things that took up most of my spare time, such as homework and a part-time job (okay, boys may have taken up just a weensy bit of that time too). I got married. I had two daughters. I got divorced. Eventually, I got married again. We bumbled along day to day and thoughts of yarn never entered my head. Until something happened that completely changed things. I got pregnant again.

Everyone knows that when a woman is pregnant she gets odd cravings. Some want to gorge on pickles every waking moment while others get up in the middle of the night to raid the Marmite jar. I didn't get food cravings. Never have, much to my disappointment - who wouldn't want a cast-iron excuse to indulge whenever the fancy takes you? I did however have other cravings.

As soon as that little blue line appeared in the test window I started mooning over yarn. I didn't even realise I was doing it at first. I'd walk along the High Street and slow as I approached the yarn store, a shop that had hitherto held no interest for me. I'd smile and sigh at all the tiny jumpers and bootees so fetchingly displayed, pat my tummy and move on. Gradually I moved from staring in the window to going in and fondling the yarns, earning myself a few strange looks from the staff who you'd think would be used to that kind of thing, working in a yarn shop and all. Finally, when I caught myself leafing through the few (the very few) crochet patterns on sale and trying to remember which stitch was which I decided I had to give in to my base urges. I grabbed a pattern, hook and ball of yarn, paid and scuttled home to give it a go.

The resulting baby jacket was not an unqualified success. For a start it was green. Now don't get me wrong, green is actually my favourite colour - just not this green. But if you can't use proper girl or boy colours because you have a husband who is adamant that he doesn't want to know baby's gender, and if you don't want to use white then you don't have a whole lot of choices left. Secondly it was 100% unashamed, squeaky acrylic because at the time I didn't know any better. Still, every chain, single and double crochet was made with a mother's love and that's what counts - who cared if it had the elasticity of cardboard and the cuffs were so tight that those tiny wrinkly hands practically had to be threaded through one finger at a time?

Baby cared, that's who. All ready to leave the maternity hospital, bundled up in her lovely new jacket that mummy had so lovingly made by hand, Mhara decided to tell the world what she thought of her going-home outfit by throwing up. Not just a little, oh no, this was an entire feed all down the front. Not that I minded - by this time I was well and truly re-hooked on crochet and acrylic, while it may be stiff, squeaky and static-prone is at least machine-wash.

Since that baby jacket I've discovered merino wool, and silk, and cashmere. And all sorts of other luscious fibres that work wonderfully well with crochet, despite what some folks may believe. I've discovered different stitches, including crochet rib which was a revelation and meant that it's now much easier to get Mhara and her baby brother Rowan's hands into (and back out of) sleeves. I've even started playing around with one or two patterns of my own design - simple things like fingerless mitts, hats and hair bands which may not be big or fancy but give me a huge sense of achievement.

I love crochet. I love the organic process of using what basically boils down to some string and a hook to make a piece of fabric that can take on any shape you like. It's not structured or regimented but rather grows in front of your eyes with a fluid grace that is beautiful to watch. The same few simple stitches can be used to make a delicate, light and airy wrap or something fun and funky like the Alien Battle Helmet that is currently Rowan's favourite headgear.

Different materials can be used to stunning effect. Some beads and a spool of wire can become a bracelet or a choker in no time. Leather thong can make stylish place mats. Even something as simple as a few balls of twine from the hardware store can become a sturdy shopper that is so much better, aesthetically and environmentally, than a fistful of plastic bags.

Crochet is supremely portable. A ball of yarn and a hook take up practically no space at all and there's no worry about long pointy bits poking innocent passers-by. They can fit easily into a handbag or pocket ready to be whipped out on the bus or train, often much to the interest of fellow passengers. And when your stop looms the whole lot can be slipped away without worrying about losing stitches.

Being able to make special gifts for those near and dear is also a great source of comfort. When trouble calls my instinct is always to wonder, what can I make to help cheer him or her up? Hand-made gifts mean so much more than something picked up in a store and the rhythmic movements of hook and yarn help to relax my body and soothe my mind as I work.

Best of all though, crochet is a skill that is easy to pass on. It's going to be a few years before the babies are big enough to manipulate a hook without poking out their own eyes - or, more likely, each others' - but I'm lucky enough to have two teenage daughters as well and I taught my second daughter to crochet a few years ago. She loves to craft and has already started making up her own designs. I get such a thrill out of seeing her intent on her work and when she comes to me to show off what she's made I feel so proud of her, just as I imagine my Mum feels proud of me when I show her something new that I've made. What more could I ask for than that?

This heart shaped ornament has a history…
It will be 10 years old this Christmas season (2008). I had just returned to the USA with my two children having left a dysfunctional marriage half way around the world. I didn't leave with much other than the children. I had very little money, and a five year old daughter who was convinced that Santa couldn't find her because we had moved so far away.
I found a pretty tree, but couldn't afford the electric bill for lights on the tree, I had left all of my ornaments behind, and well that just wouldn't do. A five year old's eyes were dimming; so much loss, so much change. I needed to give her some hope. So, I got some flannel , and bought some thread, and a lace hook and crocheted until my fingers were stiff and sore… My little girl would take each ornament as it was finished and place it on the tree, saying, "The more we put the more magic for Santa."
Needless to say, Santa found her, and it snowed on Christmas Eve. They remain the favorite holiday trim in our family… Laurie Wheeler (Camanomade)

Cabled Slouch

Zuleika Lambe (Crochetzu)

MATERIALS (needed for an adult regular)

Hook sizes H(5mm) and G(4mm)
3 balls Sirdar Chunky with Wool – approx. 150 grams/200 yds/182m
Yarn needle

FINISHED MEASUREMENTS
22 inches around the hat brim
9 inches from the top of hat to brim edge (unstretched)

GAUGE
 7 dc's and 4 rows= 2 inches.

SPECIAL STITCHES

FPDC – Front Post Double Crochet:

TR – Treble Crochet:

 DC2TOG – Double Crochet Decrease (Double Crochet 2 together)

PATTERN NOTES
Ch 1 at beginning of row isn't counted as a stitch and mostly serves to avoid a visible seam.

Using a size H hook (5mm) form a loop using the magic loop method.	
Rnd 1: Ch 3, 11 dc in ring. Join with a sl st to the top of ch 3. (12)	Row 7: Ch 1, 1 dc in same st, *1 FPDC in next FPDC, "1 dc in top of same FPDC you just worked into", skip next 2 sts, 1 tr in each of the next 2 sts. Working under the previous tr's, work 1 tr in each of the missed sts. 1 dc in next st*, repeat from * to * to end. End row with cabled trebles, sl st to top of 1st dc. (84) (Directions between "..." are ONLY for row 7. For row 8-12 the dc is worked into the following st, not the FPDC)
Rnd 2: Ch 1, 2 dc in same st and in each st around. Sl st to the top of 1st dc. (24)	Row 8: Repeat row seven, except work in front of the previous trebles instead of behind them. End row with cabled trebles, sl st to top of 1st dc. (84)
Rnd 3: Ch 1, 2 dc in same st, *1 FPDC in next st, 2 dc in next st*, repeat from * to * to end. Last FPDC worked around previous rows ch 1. Sl st to the top of the 1st dc. (36)	Row 9: 9-14.) Alternate rows 7 and 8. (84)
Rnd 4: Ch 1, 2 dc in next st, *1 FPDC in next FPDC, 1 dc in next st, 2 dc in next st*; repeat from * to * to end, end row with 1 dc in base of ch 1 st. Sl st to the top of the 1st dc. (48)	Change to G hook (4mm) 15.) Ch 3, 1 dc2tog in same and next st, *1 dc in each of the next 5 sts, 1 dc2tog in next 2 sts*, . Repeat from * to *, to the end. Sl st to top of 1st dc. (72)
Rnd 5: Ch 1, 2 dc in next st, *1 FPDC in next FPDC, 1 dc in each of the next 2 sts, 2 dc in next st*; repeat from * to * to end, end row with 1 dc in ch 1 st. Sl st to top of 1st dc. (60)	16-17.) Ch 1, 1 sc in same st and in each st around. Sl st to 1st sc. (72)
Rnd 6" Ch 1, 2 dc in next st, *1 FPDC in next FPDC, 1 dc in each of the next 3 sts, 2 dc in next st*; repeat from * to * to end, end row with 1 dc in ch 1 st. Sl st to the top of 1st dc. (72)	Finish off and weave in ends. *Crochetzu would love to hear from you if you have questions or comments about this pattern, please contact her at http://www.hobbyzu.com/*

Phoenix Mitts

By Julia Vaconsin (aka jujustrickt) ©2008

This is a wonderfully delicate and lightweight pair of fingerless mittens that'll keep your wrists warm through all seasons. They are perfect to show off a nice lace weight yarn in a color and composition of your choice.

Yarn : Malabrigo Lace (100% Baby Merino Wool, aprox. 470 yards/50g), color 102 Sealing Wax: 1 skein (30 g should be enough for a pair)

Hook: Steel crochet hook size 4 (1.75 mm). Adjust hooks size to obtain the correct gauge.

Gauge: 5 shells and 14 rows over treble shell pattern = 10 cm (4 inches)

Notes: This pattern uses US terminology.

Cuff

To begin: Ch 16.

Row 1: Sc in 2nd ch from hook and in each across, turn. – *15 sc*

Row 2: Ch 1, sc tbl across, turn.

Repeat row 2, 54 more times

Fold cuff in half, sl st across cast on chain and last row at the same time.

Turn cuff inside out (so that seam is on the inside).

Wrist: *Start working in treble shell pattern:*

Set-up rd: Ch 4, tr 3 in first row end, *sk 3 row ends, sc in next row end, sk 3 row ends, tr 7 in next row end, repeat from * to last 7 row ends, sk 3 row ends, sc 1 in next row end, sk 3 row ends, tr 3 in first row end, join to rd with a sc in top of ch-4. *(= 7 shells)*

Rd 1: *tr 7 in next sc, sc 1 in 4th st of next 7-st-shell, repeat from * around.

Rd 2: Ch 4, tr 3 in 1st sc of prev rd, sc 1 in 4th st of next 7-st-shell, *tr 7 in next sc, sc in 4th st of next 7-st-shell, repeat from * to end of rd, tr 3 in sc at beg of rd, join to rd with a sl st in ch 4

Part A: Cuff and Wrist (make 2)

Chart A

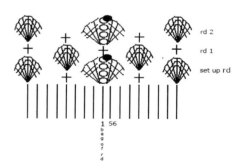

Repeat last 2 rounds for pattern until piece measures about 12 cm (4.5 inches), ending with round 2.

Thumb:

Rd 1 *(see also Chart C)*: Ch 4, tr 3 in first sc, sc in 4th tr of 7-tr-shell, tr 7 in next sc, skip next 6 7-st-shells, sc 1 in 4th st of next shell, tr 7 in next sc, sc 1 in 4th st of next shell, tr 3 in first sc of rd, join rd with a sl st in top of ch-4.

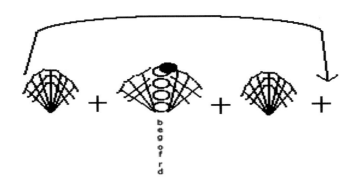

Work 3 rows even in pattern, ending the last rd with a sl st (rather than a sc). Fasten off.

Palm:

Reattach yarn at palm opening next to thumb. New beginning of round is here.

Rd 1 *(Rd 1 of Chart A)*: Sc 1 in 4th st of first shell, *tr 7 in next sc, sc 1 in 4th st of next shell, repeat from * around, work a 7-st-shell in base of thumb, sc 1 in top of ch-4. *(= 7 shells)*

Work 6 rounds even, ending the last rd with a sl st (rather than a sc). Fasten off.

Weave in ends, close any holes that might have occurred between the thumb and the palm while doing so.

Wash and block as desired.

The Strands of Heritage

By Elizabeth Denton (tsel)

Margaret Bade, my grandmother, came to America a few years after World War I with her two young children. Her husband had decided that Luxemburg, sandwiched neatly between France and Germany, was not a safe place for his family. So after working and saving up enough money for them to travel second-class across the Atlantic, he had the family join him in Harvey, an industrial boomtown south of Chicago. Unfortunately, my great-grandfather died of a lung disease and left my great-grandma alone during the depression with two children. When the aid society she applied to asked her what she knew how to do, she brought out samples of her schoolwork – and that was the beginning of her career. In the early 1900s in Luxemburg, women were instructed in domestic tasks, including sewing and embroidery, and Margaret seemed to be particularly skilled at it. The aid society got her a job working for a fancy dressmaker, and she was able to support her family throughout the depression as a single parent.

Unfortunately, my great-grandfather died of a lung disease and left my great-grandma alone during the depression with two children. When the aid society she applied to asked her what she knew how to do, she brought out samples of her schoolwork – and that was the beginning of her career. In the early 1900s in Luxemburg, women were instructed in domestic tasks, including sewing and embroidery, and Margaret seemed to be particularly skilled at it. The aid society got her a job working for a fancy dressmaker, and she was able to support her family throughout the depression as a single parent.

We aren't completely sure if Margaret learned crocheting in school, or afterwards, but she certainly could do it by the 1940s. My mother has a pair of lace gloves that she made – and that would have been fashionable at the end of the depression. They are very clearly fine crochet work – and are a remarkable sample of the talent of an equally remarkable woman.

Margaret continued crocheting well into her 90s, when she made my sister's baby blanket using a diagonal box stitch. My mother was surprised by how quickly she could turn out that stitch, even at her advanced age.

I have very clear memories of my great-grandmother, who was in many ways my childhood best friend. I was devastated when she passed away as I entered my teens, and I still miss her. Learning to crochet as an adult has been an important way to reconnect with this amazing woman. Among my hooks are some of hers, and I can see with certainty the way our lives are tied together.

Broomstick Lace Wrap

By Tracie Barrett (traciecrochets)

© 2008 Fibers By Tracie

Editor's note: A more challenging pattern...are you up for it? I double dog dare you! Come on it'll be fun!

Notes:

- Wrap is worked in one direction, finished off, and then thread is reattached to base chain and worked in opposite direction for an equal length.
- Pay careful attention to instructions at end of rows. Some rows you will turn the work and others you will not.
- Be careful when putting the loops on the pin to not pull too tight. You will need to be able to insert your hook through the loops while they're on the pin.

Materials:
- Approx. 2000 yards lace weight rayon or Size 10 cotton E / 3.5mm crochet hook Tapestry Needle

Wooden dowels for broomstick pins: 1/2" diameter and 5/8" diameter - for ease of working on dowels, be sure to lightly sand the dowels before use. Also, tapering one end makes it a lot easier to get the loops on and off.

Chain (ch)
Single Crochet (sc)
Double Crochet (dc)
Yarn over (yo)
Slip Stitch (sl st)

Double Base Chain: Ch 2, YO, insert hook into side and back loop of first chain, YO, pull up a loop, YO, pull through 1 loop (ch made), YO pull through 2 loops on hook, YO pull through 2 loops (dc made), * YO, insert hook into side and back loop of ch just made, YO, pull up a loop, YO pull through 1 loop, YO and pull through 2 loops on hook, YO pull through last 2 loops on hook; rep from * for specified number of double base chains.

Gauge:
28 dc x 13 rows in pattern = 4" (Gauge is not critical to this project)

Finished Size: 16" x 48"

Make a double base chain of 120. Turn

Row 1: **Ch 1, sc in each st across. DO NOT TURN**

Row 2: **Pull up a loop and place on larger pin, * insert hook into back loop of next st and pull up a loop and place on pin; Repeat from * to last stitch. <u>DO NOT TURN</u>**

Row 3: **Insert hook through first 6 loops on pin, YO, pull loop through and ch 1 to lock loops, 6 sc across top of loops, * insert hook through next 6 loops, place 6 sc across top of loops; Repeat from * across to last stitch, turn.**

Row 4: **Ch 2 (counts as dc here and throughout), dc in each sc across. Turn**

Row 5: **Ch 1, sc in each st across. DO NOT TURN.**

Row 6: **Pull up a loop and place on smaller pin, * insert hook into back loop of next st and pull up a loop and place on pin; Repeat from * to last stitch. DO NOT TURN**

Row 7: **Insert hook through first 3 loops on pin, YO, pull loop through and ch 1 to lock loops, 3 sc across top of loops, * insert hook through next 3 loops, place 3 sc across top of loops; Repeat from * across to last stitch, turn**

Row 8: **Ch 2, dc in each sc across. Turn**

Rows 9-72: **Repeat rows 1-8 nine more times**

Row 73: **Ch 1, sc in first st and each st across. Finish off. With RS facing, attach thread to other side of base chain.**

Repeat Rows 1-73. Do not finish off, do not turn.

Edging: Round 1: **Ch 1, sc evenly around piece, placing 3 sc in corners, sc in end of each row and 3 sc around 2 outer loops of each broomstick row. Join with sl st to beginning sc.**

HOOK-A-LICIOUS YOGINI SPRING CARRY ALL

(aka "CROCHETED BITCHINESS" SUPER TOTE)

--Yavanna Coulter Reynolds (aka. Datenshi)

> *"I think crocheted bitchiness would be totally fierce couture crochet. Something over –the- top and fabulous, very "Devil Wears Prada" does crochet. It would be artistic, and beautiful beyond words and scream, I'm the shiznet! It would be the item so beautiful that others will try to copy it, yet so illusive that no one would succeed at doing so."*
>
> **--datenshi (myself) from a CLF thread titled "Can you crochet bitchiness?"**

Materials:

Yarn: Reynolds Saucy. Worsted weight 100% mercerized cotton. 185 yrds/100g.

Gauge: (for yarn substitution) on size 7 needles, 20 sts =4". 20-21 sts wide by 8-9sts tall=4" in hdc (half double crochet) when properly blocked.

Colors:

- MC—color 869 (lt. blue) 5 skeins. (925 yrds)
- CC—color 110 (lt. green) 2.33 skeins. (420 yrds)
- CCC—color 396 (dusty rose) ½ skein (93yrds)

I created this in contrasting colors to show off the different stitch patterns and techniques. If you would like to do this all in one color you'll need 1438yrds or 7.75 skeins of Reynolds Saucy. Other stiff cotton yarns can also be appropriate for this pattern. It might also look beautiful in hemp, jute, or another yarn with a stiff hand and not too much drape. As it is, the cotton is almost too drapy.

Hooks: 1 US size B1 (2.25mm), 1US size C2 (2.75mm) hook. Aluminum is recommended.

Other Notions:

- 2-7/8" half dome buttons
- 4-5/8"(15mm) half dome buttons
- 1-¾"purse magnet
- sewing needle
- button hole or embroidery thread (to match MC)
- Stitch markers or safety pins

Specialty Stitch Patterns or Techniques:

 --**Datenshi's Lazy Chrysanthemum lace motif** (see chart)

--**Datenshi's Not so Lazy Chrysanthemum Lace**

<table>
<tr><td>

Abbreviations:

ch: chain

st(s): Stitch(es)

sl st: slip stitch

sc: single crochet

dc: double crochet

</td></tr>
</table>

CREATING BAG BOTTOM:

FOUNDATION: Using a size C hook, ch 60sts. Turn to back of ch, sc into each butt loop starting at 3rd st from hook continuing to end of chain.
Slst into knot at beginning of ch to end.

RND 1: Ch 1. SC into each ch st along top side *(3sc in corner st). SC in each st on backside, repeat *.

RND 2: Ch 2. Hdc in each sc along topside edge *(in the 3 edge sts: 2hdc in corner st, 1hdc, 2 hdc in corner st). Hdc in each sc on backside to corner. Repeat * for last 3 sts. Sl into 2 ch to end rnd.

RND 3: Ch 2. Hdc in each st on side. *(In the 5 edge sts: 2hdc in 2sts, hdc in 3rd st, 2hdc in last 2sts). Hdc in all sts on opposite side. In last 5 sts. Repeat * for last 5 sts. Sl into 2ch to end rnd.

RND 4: Ch 2. Hdc in each st on side. *(in 9 edge sts: 2hdc, 3hdc, 1 hdc in next 5 sts, 3hdc, 2hdc). Hdc in all sts on opposite side. Repeat * for last 9 sts. Sl into 2ch to end rnd.

RND 5: Ch 2. Hdc in each st on side. *(in 13 edge/side sts: 2hdc in 3sts, hdc in next 7 sts, 2hdc in last 3 sts). Hdc in all sts along back side. Repeat * for last 13 sts. Sl st into 2ch to end rnd.

RND 6: Ch 2. Hdc in each st on side. *(in 15 edge/side sts: 2hdc in 3sts, hdc in next 9 sts, 2hdc in last 3 sts). Hdc in all sts along back side. 17 sts before end, Repeat * for next 13 sts. Hdc in last 2 sts. Sl st into 2ch to end rnd.

RND 7: Ch 2. Hdc in each st on side. *(in 19 edge/side sts: 2hdc in 3sts, hdc in next 13sts, 2hdc in last 3 sts). Continue as before to corner. 21 sts before end, Repeat * for next 19 sts. Hdc in last 2 sts. Sl st into 2ch to end rnd.

RND 8: Ch 2. Hdc in each st on side. *(in 21 edge/side sts: 2hdc in 1st st, 3 hdc in next st, 2hdc, hdc in following 15sts, 2hdc, 3hdc, 2hdc). Continue as before to corner. 25 sts before end, Repeat * for next 21 sts. Hdc in last 4 sts. Sl st into 2ch to end rnd.

RND 9: Ch 2. Hdc in each st on side. *(in 23 edge/side sts: 2hdc in 2sts, hdc in following 19sts, 2hdc in 2 sts). Continue as before to corner. 29 sts before end, Repeat * for next 23 sts. Hdc in last 6 sts. Sl st into 2ch to end rnd.

RND 10: Ch 2. Hdc in each st on side. *(in 27 edge/side sts: 2hdc in 3sts, hdc in following 21sts, 2hdc in 3 sts). Continue as before to corner. 33 sts before end, Repeat * for next 27 sts. Hdc in last 6 sts. Sl st into 2ch to end rnd.

RND 11: Ch 2. Hdc in each st on side until piece begins to curve. *(in 31 edge/side sts: 2hdc in 3sts, hdc in following 25sts, 2hdc in 3 sts). Continue as before to corner. 38 sts before end, Repeat * for next 31 sts. Hdc in last 7 sts. Sl st into 2ch to end rnd.

RND 12: Ch 2. Hdc in each st on side until piece begins to curve. *(in 33 edge/side sts: 3hdc in 1st st, 2hdc in next st, hdc in following 29sts, 2hdc, 3hdc). Continue as before to corner. 40 sts before end, Repeat * for next 33 sts. Hdc in last 7 sts. Sl st into 2ch to end rnd.

CHART 1: BASE OF BAG

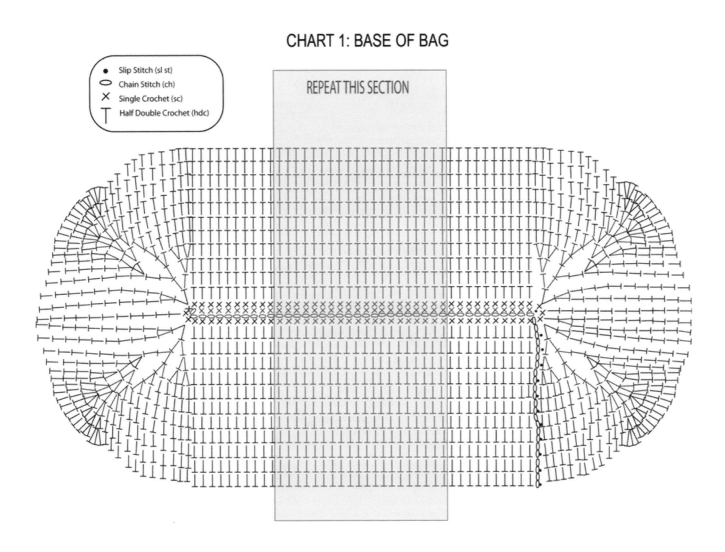

- You have completed the very bottom foundation for your bag. At this point, depending on the stiffness of the yarn used, and how tightly crocheted the project is, you may want to block the piece before moving on to the bag sides. Block lightly with steam (if appropriate) at the recommended heat setting for the yarn you are using. Pull and stretch the panel until it is a balanced rectangle with rounded corners. **At this point, after blocking, your piece should measure about 6 1/4" wide by 18" long.**

TURNING THE CORNER:

- With correct side of the fabric (bag's outer bottom) facing down, sl over the last 7 sts completed, bringing you to the corner of the fabric. This will be the new starting place for your round.

- Working from this point, ch 3, dc in each st around edge of work, frequently pausing to push new stitches toward the inside of the bag, encouraging the bag to grow skyward. Sl into 3 ch to end rnd. You should notice a very subtle curve of the sts towards the inside, creating the beginnings of a "bowl"

WORKING BAG SIDES:

RND 1:   Ch 2. Hdc around entire piece. Sl into ch to end rnd,

RND 2:   Yo, insert hook into last st worked, yo, pull loop through but do not complete st, yo, insert hook into next st, yo, pull new loop through all 5 loops on hook—1 st hdc decreased. Hdc entire rnd, hdc dec each consecutive corner (3 more corners). Sl st into first hdc dec st to end rnd.

RND 3-5:   Ch 2. Hdc all sts. Sl st into ch to end row.

RND 6:   Ch3. Dc all sts. Sl st into chain to end.

RND 7-10: Repeat rnds 2-4

Lace detail—Lazy Chysanthemum fan border

Lace Insert:--Datenshi's Lazy Chrysanthemum

RND 1:   Ch 1, sc in all sts. Sl to end Rnd.

RND 2:   Ch 3. Sk 1, hdc in next st. *(ch1, sk1, hdc in next st). Repeat * around entire piece. Ch 1. Sl st into ch to end rnd.

RND 3:   Ch 1. Sc in first 3 sts. * (5hdc into next st, sc into next 4 sts, hdc into following st, sc 4 sts). Repeat * to end. Sl st into ch to close rnd.

RND 4:   Ch 1 [*(2 Trc into 1st st. Ch 1) repeat * for each hdc st in fan (10 trc total). Sk next 4 sts. Sl st into next st. Sk 4 sts.] Repeat [] pattern around entire piece. Sl into ch to close rnd.

RND 5:   Ch 7 *(sc into the 2 trc at top of 1st fan. Ch 5, Trc into st directly between fans sts, ch 5). Repeat * all along edge, sl st int 3rd ch st to end rnd.

RND 6:   Ch 3 sk 1 *(hdc, ch1 sk1). Repeat * along entire piece ending with sl st into 2 ch.

RND 7:   Ch 1. Sc in each st, sl st to end rnd.

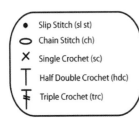

	Slip Stitch (sl st)
●	Chain Stitch (ch)
⬭	Single Crochet (sc)
✕	Half Double Crochet (hdc)
┬	Triple Crochet (trc)

CHART 2:   Datenshi's Lazy Chrysanthemum

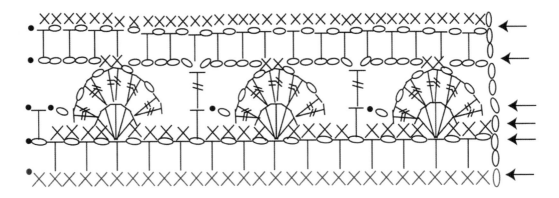

FINISHING THE BASE:

(Ch 2. Hdc entire rnd. Sl st into ch to end.) repeat for next rnd.

WORKING THE STRAPS:

- Starting at beginning of round, find the four corners of the piece and place a marker in each corner. The long sides should be 115 sts and the short sides 41 sts long.

- Count 33 sts from corner. Place marker. Count 9 sts from last marker, pm. Count 30 sts from last marker, pm, count another 9 sts from marker, place marker. Repeat on other side of bag starting at corner and going along longer edge of bag. The 9 sts between the sets of markers will be the straps.

- Join yarn in first marker from corner. Work the 9 sts between this marker and the next following the instructions that follow:

STRAP ROW 1:   Ch 2, hdc in each of the 9 sts. Ch 2 turn.
STRAP ROW 2:   Hdc in each of the 9 sts. Ch 2 turn.
STRAP ROW 3-4:   Repeat rows 1 & 2. End row 4 with a ch 3 instead of ch 2.
STRAP ROW 5:   Ch 3, dc in each of the 9 sts. Ch 2, turn.
STRAP ROW 6:   Hdc 9 sts, ch 2, turn

- **REPEAT ROWS 1-6 another 18 times (total of 19 times).** Turn, complete one additiona hdc row as before. Holding strap in place between next two markers, correct side to correct side, working with both sets of stitches facing up, sc through both pieces, treating both the strap and the bag stitches as one st. Continue to crochet these stitches in this manner until all 9 stitches between the marker have been crocheted.

- Work around the edge of the completed strap by working hdc sts sideways, up and around the inside edge of the strap, with at least one stitch in each row. Sl st into each sts between the strap ends and across the joined edge of the strap and bag, reinforcing the connection.

- Hdc in each row around outer edge, bind off.

- **REPEAT INSTRUCTIONS FOR MAKING A STRAP** working rows 1-6, 19 times.
- Work outer edge of strap with hdc sts as before. Bind off at end.
- Restart reinforcement edge on inside of strap. Work hdc sts along inner edge. Bind off.
- Work outer edge of strap in same manner. Bind off.

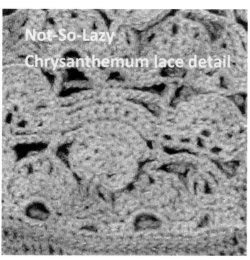

Not-So-Lazy
Chrysanthemum lace detail

PANELS BETWEEN THE STRAPS—Datenshi's Not-so-lazy chrysanthemum lace
- Begin working lace pattern between straps in CC following lace pattern and beginning in lower right hand corner.
ROW 1:   Join yarn by connecting into lower right hand corner in space between straps. Sc 32 times. Sl into strap.
ROW 2:   Ch 1 *(sc into next 3 sts, Ch 5 sk 2 sts, sc). Repeat * 4 ,pre times. SC int last 2 sts. Sl st into strap
ROW 3:   Ch 1 * (sc into next 2 sts, ch 2 sk 4, sc into 3rd st in chain, ch 2 sk 3 sts into next st, chain 1 sk 2 sts, 7 sc into next 5 ch loop, working into the loop and not directly into the sts. Ch 2 sk 4). Repeat *. Sc into 3rd st in chain, ch 2 sk 3 sts, sc into next 2 sts, sl st into strap to end row.
ROW 4:   Ch 1, sc [sc into nex st, ch 2, hdc into sc, ch 2, sc into next sc st, sk ch st *(2hdc into1st sc, ch 1, sk next st) repeat * 3 more times. Sk ch st]. Repeat [] once, sc into next st. Ch 2, hdc into sc st. Ch 2, sc into last 2 sc sts. Sl st into strap to end row.

ROW 5:   Ch 1, sc into next 2 sts, ch 3, dc into hdc, ch 4, sl st into next sc st. *(2dc into next set of 2 hdc sts, ch1) repeat * 3 times. [sl st into next sc st. Ch 4 dc into next hdc st. Ch 5. Sl st into top of dc st. Sc 7 times into loop created by ch. Turn, ch 1 (hdc, ch 1) into each sc of loop, turn, ch 1, 2 hdc ch 1 into each hdc st, sl st into next sc ch 4 dc into next hdc st. Repeat * 4 more times into next fan. Slst into following sc, ch 4. Dc into next hdc st, ch 3, sc into last 2 sts, sl st into srap to end row

ROW 6:   Ch 1, sc into next 2 sts, ch 3, sc into dc st, ch 5, dc into center top ch of fan between sets of 2 dc sts, ch 2m sc into 2nd 2 hdc cluster in large motif, sc in next 10 sts around edge of motif. Ch 2, dc into ch at top of next fan, ch 5 sc into next dc st, ch 3 sk 3sts, sc in next 2 sts. Sl st into strap to end row.

ROW 7: Sl st 3 more times moving up the side of the strap. Ch 4, sk 5 sts, sc, ch 5, hdc into next dc st, ch 2 sk 4, sc into next 7 sts, ch 2, hdc into next dc st, ch 5, sc into next sc st, ch 4 sl st into strap.

ROW 8: Sl st 2 more times moving up side of strap. Ch 2 sk2. *(Hdc in next st, ch 1 sk1) repeat * 3 more times. Hdc into next hdc st, sc into next 11 sts, hdc in next hdc st, ch 1 sk 1.

ROW 9: Ch 1 sc into next 3 sts. Sk 1, hdc 5 times into next st. Sk 1 sc into next 5 sts, ch 3 sk 3, sc into next 5 sts, ch 3 sk 3, sc into next 5 sts, sk 1, 5 hdc into next st, sk 1, sc into last 3 sts, sl st into srap.

ROW 10: Ch 1 sk 3 *(2 dc ch 1 into next 5 hdc, sk 3). Hdc, ch 5 sk 6, sc into next 3 sts, ch 5 sk 5 hadc in next st, ch 1 sk 3. Repeat *, ch 1 sl st into strap.

ROW 11: Sl 3 more times up side of strip. Ch 3 sk 7, sc, sh 4 sk 10, Trc into hdc before next ch set. Ch 5, sk 5, sc in next 3 sts. Ch 5 sk 5, Trc into 1st hdc after chain, chain 4 sk 10 sts, sc, ch 3 sk 7 sl into strap to end.

ROWS 12-21: Repeat rows 2-11

ROW 22: Ch 1, sc in next 32 sts, slst into strap to end row.

ROW 23: Sk 1, hdc (ch 1, sk 1, hdc). Repeat across piece, ch 1 sl st into strap. Binde off to end.

Repeat rows 1-23 on other side between strap ends.

- ● Slip Stitch (sl st)
- ◯ Chain Stitch (ch)
- ✕ Single Crochet (sc)
- T Half Double Crochet (hdc)
- T Double Crochet (dc)
- ‡ Triple Crochet (trc)

CHART 3: Datenshi's Not-So-Lazy Chrysanthemum

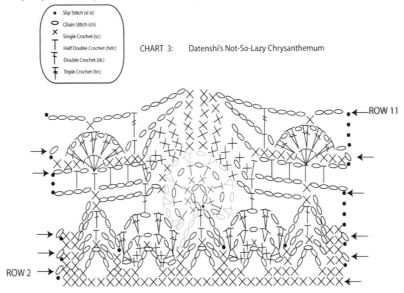

ROW 11

ROW 2

CONNECTING THE SIDES—Japanese picot lantern mesh stitch

ROW 1: Join yarn in strap corner on the outside left corner of strap. SC each st between straps. You should have 110 sts total (you may need to add more sts to the beginning and/or end of this row to reach this number. 110 sts are necessary for completing the pattern.

ROW 2: Ch 5 sk 5, sc into next st *(ch 5 sk 4, dc in next st, ch 5 sk 4, sc) into last 5 sts. Ch 5 sk 5, sl into strap to end row. Ch 1 and turn.

ROW 3: *(sc 6 times onto chain, sk into sc st, ch 3 sl into sc (picot), sc 3 times onto next ch, ch 4 moving backwards along piece. Sl st into st created 3 sts before current picot.. Moving forwards along pic, 5 sc onto chain just created. Continuing forward, sc into ch below to join and secure new ch. Sc two more times on chain, sc into dc st). Repeat * across piece (10 times) ending with sl st into strap. Ch 1 and turn.

ROW 4: Sc into 1st sc st. *(ch5, 6 dc into 3rd center st of arch above picot. Ch 5, sc into center st between picot arches). Repeat across piece another 9 times. In last 5 sts end with ch 5 sk 5, sc, sl st, ch 1 and turn,.

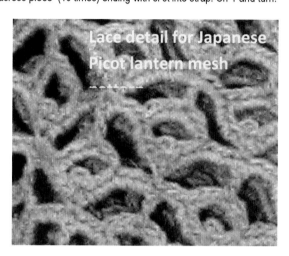

Lace detail for Japanese Picot lantern mesh

ROW 5—SC into ch 4 times, ch 2. Moving backwards, sl into strap at point 3 sts higher than entrance point. Ch 1, moving forward, sc 3 times into new ch, sc into previous ch to secure arch, sc 2 more times in ch. Sc into dc st *(6 sc into ch, 1 sc into sc st below, 3 ch picot (ch 3, sl st). Sc 3 times into ch st. Ch 4. Moving backwards sl st 3 sts before picot, moving forward sc 5 times into new ch loop. Sc into previous ch to secure. Sc 2 more times into previous ch, sc into dc st). Repeat * across piece , stopping at last 5 ch loop. Sc 6 times into last 5 ch. Sl st into strap.Sl 3 more times up side, ch 2, sl st into strap 4 times total, moving up 3 spaces.

ROW 6: Ch 5 sk 6, sc into next st *(ch 5 sk 4, dc in next st, ch 5 sk 4, sc) into last 5 sts. Ch 5 sk 5, sl into strap to end row. Ch 1 and turn.

ROWS 7-9: Repeat rows 3-5

ROW 10-13: Repeat rows 6-9.

ROW 14:   Repeat row 6

ROW 15:   Repeat row 7. At the end of row, instead of moving up strap 3 spaces (total of 4 sl sts), move up only one additional space, sl st one place up strap. Ch 1, turn.

ROW 16:   Sk 1 *(hdc ch 1 sk 1)repeat * across piece. Sl st into end, bind off.

REPEAT ROWS 1-16 for OTHER SIDE OF BAG.

Finishing the edge

RND 1:   starting in the location where you had just finished your lace panel, *(sc around post on back of strap so sts are only visible on back of strap, sl st in each st on way to next strap). Repeat * all along strap. Sl st into 1st st in rnd to end rnd.

RND 2:   Ch2, hdc in all sts. Sl st into ch to end.

RND 3:   Ch 3, Dc in all sts. Sl st into ch to end.

RND 4:   Flip bag around so that the correct side of the bag is facing you. Work a sl st into each st, creating a pretty, sturdy edge.

ADDING BUTTON PLACKETS

There are 5 button plackets. 4 are functional button/loop style. One is just a flap that will close and open by use of a purse magnet. These plackets serve the dual purpose of being decorative and also helping the bag keep its shape when it is almost empty.

Placement of the 4 plackets:

- Find the four edges of the bag. Fold bag in such a way that the front and back edges meet. The back edge crease is where the individual plackets will be placed. The button will be placed just inside of the crease on the front.
- The top plackets will also stretch from the back of the bag to the front of the bag. Only they will be crocheted directly into the purse edge instead of on the seam.

Instructions for 4 smaller plackets:

- Join yarn into necessary location (back side "seam" for bottom plackets, upper corner for upper plackets) and sc into 7 sts on edge. (ch 2, turn, hdc in each st) repeat * 6 times, ch 8, sl st into last st in row. Work 10 sc sts around edge of 8 ch loop. Continue sc around edge of piece. Sl st into base of placket to other side. Sc around outer edge, bind off. Repeat for remaining plackets.

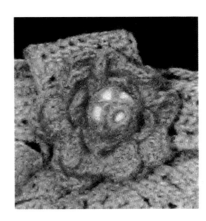

Instructions for larger center placket:

- Find space about 10 sts wide exactly between straps. On back side, join yarn and crocht 10 sts (ch 2, hdc 10 sts) Repeat 10 times. Sc in all sts, continue to sc around edge of piece, working sc sts into the base and continuing around the other edge. Sl into first sc to join.

IRISH CROCHET BUTTON CENTER FLOWERS

I wanted to make my buttons functional and beautiful. So I built Irish crochet flowers around them.

LARGE FLOWER BUTTONS:

- Build this flower on the larger of the 2 dome button sizes.
- Ch 5 in CCC color. Sl st into beginning of ch to form a ring. Sc 8 times into this ring. Ch 2, sk 1, (dc ch 1 sk 1) around entire piece. Sl st into 2 ch to end rnd.
- Ch 1 ,sc in all sts
- Place button into cup of sts, face down. This may be difficult at this stage. You may want to work halfway through the next row before inserting your button.
- Ch 1, sc2tog (sc two together). Repeat until all stitches have been worked.
- With button inside sts, sc around edge one more time to secure button placement.
- Ch 3, sc into ring at base of button. Repeat 3 times, forming 4 loops.
- (2hd, 1dc, 1trc, 1dc, 2hdc) onto each loop, forming petal. Repeat for each loop.
- Sl st into first loop. *(Ch 3, sl st around post of trc st in first petal. Ch 3, sl st into space between petals.) Repeat * into each petal around piece.
- (2hdc, 2dc, 1 trc, 2dc, 2hdc) into each chain loop. Sl st into 1st petal to end rnd.

- Ch 5, sl behind post between petals . Repeat 4 times for a total of 5 loops.
- (2hd, 2dc,2 trc, 1dtrc (double triple crochet)) work into each loop. Bind off to end.

LARGE FLOWER BUTTONS:

- Build this flower on the smaller of the 2 dome button sizes.
- Ch 3 in CCC color. Sl st into beginning of ch to form a ring. Sc 6 times into this ring, sl st to end rnd. Ch 3, sk 1, (dc ch 1) around entire piece. Sl st into 3ch to end rnd.
- Ch 1, sc2tog (sc two together). Repeat until all stitches have been worked. When you are halfway around this rnd, slip button into pocket created by sts.
- (ch 5 sts, sl st into ring at base of buton. Repeat 4 times to form 5 loops. Hdc into each loop 8 times . Sl st. to end.

.

FINAL TOUCHES

all buttons , snaps, or magnets to bag using matching sewing thread and a hand sewing needle

Quick tip: for ends that just won't stay woven in, try applying some clear nail polish!

8- Plied and Conquer
By Alia Smith (Crotcheteer)

It started as a lark.

Two days before Christmas and the household was in that lull between "Oh my God, how will we ever get all of this taken care of?" and "Okay, can it be Christmas now?" The breath that everyone takes when all the guests have arrived and someone is making popcorn between the second and third airings of How the Grinch Stole Christmas. The ingredients for Christmas Dinner were listed, purchased and put away after the obligatory twice-checked list. All should have been well. Right?

Nope. The proverbial comforts and joys were elusive on so many levels that a Slinky and I could have had hours of good clean fun. I had quit smoking less than a month before and despite all assurances that the nicotine was out of my system, I still felt as cagey as a Sasquatch at a Beautician's convention. Even if I hadn't quit smoking, I just don't wait well and I never have - so waiting for Christmas was a little more than my jangling receptors could take.

Finally, after the fifth square of peanut butter fudge, I queasily asked my girlfriend for a ball of yarn and a crochet hook. She is a masterful knitter but told me that when it came to crochet, I was on my own. I took them anyway; thinking that at the very least the attempt would burn up a few hours of what my schedule told me was "Teeth-Grinding" between four and seven, followed by "Lint Picking Lessons" after dinner.

My first attempts were abysmal failures but somewhere between the third pass at chaining 25 and then turning to begin another row, it got personal. As the pile of haphazard chains and knotted yarn balls on the coffee table grew, so did my resolve to own this yarn and make it bend to my will.

On the train to and from New York City, I tried. During several movies, I tried. Dreams that should have had sugarplums in them instead had pirouetting yarn balls and a crochet hook jousting match.

While the rest of the house slept off the turkey, I sat in front of a laptop watching videos of disembodied hands perform this strange dance between string and stick. Frame by frame, playing each step back, I mimicked them. But I wasn't obsessed. No, I wasn't. No. I. Wasn't.

Then suddenly, as if out of nowhere, a chain was made, and then…a row…and then…another row. Wait, I thought to myself. Am I doing this? I'm doing this. I'm DOING THIS!! Crochet, dear sweet crochet, you are my bitch! (I'll pause a moment while you imagine the crochet hook-in-fist that Winona Ryder will raise when Hollywood makes a movie out of this.)

Over the following week, I read, researched, asked questions, and –by God- entered my name on the waiting list for Ravelry.

Amazingly! Miraculously! Car rides were about the crocheting I could do on the way rather than the destination. Appointments that ran late were tolerated, even welcomed. Oh yes, I was on the verge of a hot, sexy infatuation with yarn which hoped would settle into a comfortable Sunday morning kind of love.

I had no idea how important crocheting would become.

Life was good. Well, tolerable anyway, but since the sun first rose on the very first day there have been good times and bad times and our character is shown in how we handle both.

In the New Year, my son's behavior escalated from annoying and perplexing to defiant and dangerous. Crocheting saw me through many long evenings racking my brain for solutions. It saw me through lunch hours where I wondered if I would be getting a call from the school or the bus driver.

In early February, it became clear that the things I had been seeing in him were not classic teenage rebellion. There was something very wrong and I couldn't wait any longer to act.

I remember vividly that I had a crochet hook and a skein of tan Red Heart Super Saver in my lap while I sat waiting for my son to come out of a crisis counselor's office. They were there when she agreed with me that he should be admitted to the hospital for psychiatric evaluation. They were there when I sat dazedly on the couch later that evening after kissing him goodbye and hearing intake counselor lock the heavy doors behind me.

I still have the scarf I made that day. You can actually see the places where the stitches mirrored my own zigzagging of emotion.

He's in residential treatment now and crochet allows me to deal with not knowing what will become of my brilliant, sensitive, and funny boy. I do know that at this point the best and most helpful thing I can do is get out of the way and let the people who know how to help him, do so.

I figure that at the very least, I can make sure he stays warm. And I can do it without smoking. That's something, isn't it?

Note from the Big Cheese:
When I first read this article I cried. When she sent the accompanying photo I cried a second time. I looked at each row of that sanity saving scarf, and thought, *"How can anyone put down something like this…"*

There are a lot of emotions visible in that scarf: worry, pain, anger, frustration, but most of all, there is love. Love being the basis for all those other emotions.

We can achieve greatness showing our best work, but I think we can achieve infamy by showing our honest work. Honestly, for some of us, crochet is a way to make it through the agonizing moments, days, years of our lives.

I think we've all made a few projects just like this scarf.

Power to the hooks and the hands that wield them!

Crocheted Pedicure Socks

By Deneen St. Amour (YarnsandMusings)

These socks fit my size 7 1/2 feet. You can try them on as you go along and add rounds to make them longer or take out rows to make them shorter. I made mine on the narrow size, so am changing the pattern to fit the average sized foot. Just make sure you start with an even number for the sc rounds that way you can divide it by two. I did mine with 34 sc to make it more narrow, but I've changed this to 36 sc for the part after the cuff.

Have fun with these, make the ankle part longer, change the stitch pattern around the ankle use sock weight yarn and a smaller hook have fun!

designers note: I tried these using Cascade Fixation and the elasticity of the yarn made them move around too much while wearing them my suggestion is to stick with the worsted yarn and make them snug not uncomfortable, but snug so they don't slide. I didn't have any problems using the WW yarn, just the yarn that had some "give" to it. I haven't tried it with the sock yarn yet I will, but I would try these using WW, Patons Merino would be perfect!

Crocheted Pedicure Socks

Materials

Yarn Used: Lion Brand Wool Ease (you will need a little over an ounce total for a pair of these) `

Hook size: F (3.75 mm)

Stitch Markers

Gauge: 5 st x 5 rows = 1"

**Note: you can use any type of yarn/any hook size (as long as it works with the yarn you've chosen;))Play with it and just make sure your cuff has an even number of rows to start.*

*For rounds, do not join, go in continuous rounds, use stitch marker to mark beginning of round to make things easier.

SC decrease: Draw a loop up on next stitch and then draw a loop up on the next stitch3 loops on hook, yarn over and draw through all three loops (one decrease made)

Cuff:

Row 1Chain 5, sc in 2nd chain from hook across, ch 1 and turn (4 sc)

Row 2Sc in 2nd chain from hook acrossBACK LOOP ONLY FROM HERE ON OUT FOR THE CUFF (4 st)

Do this for 42 rows total
 (if you make this larger, you will have to change your stitch count for making the socks accordingly make it an even number though). **FO and whipstitch cuff and then turn right side out.**

With back seam facing you, join yarn on left side (halfway between the back seam and front of cuff), place stitch marker and crochet evenly around (36 st), add more if you made a bigger cuff. Sc around for 2 more full rounds and then sc around front half (18 sts, ch 18 and join at stitch marker where you first started the rounds. The back of the chain and cuff opening is for the afterthought heel later on. *(depending on how many sc stitches you have here, divide it in half for afterthought heel this is if you are using fingering weight yarn, etc.)*

Sc around front and each chain (36 sts) until it measures 4" from the ribbed cuff(try on here and see how it fits). For me, this was 17 rounds. Do not finish off, continue with edging.

Toe edging Ch 1sk st, 3 dc in next st, sk st, sc in next, sk st aroundthis will make the shell edging. Sl st and fo.

Nappy Bags

By Pauline Fitzpatrick (crochet blue)

ENGLISH TERMINOLOGY USED THROUGHOUT

These bags are very easy, just make a square and a lining, then fold and sew. Follow the guidelines to create your own unique bag. But first - why Nappy Bag? Because, minus the final fold, this is how I used to fold the children's nappies[1], ready for use!

Abbreviations:

tr	treble		DK	double knitting
dc	double crochet	ss	slip stitch	
ch	chain		cm(s)	centimetre(s)
approx	approximately			

Crocheting the bag:

You can use whatever yarn you like. I used an aran weight for the large bobble bag, and DK weights for the rest. 100 grams was enough for each of the DK bags, but I needed 200 grams for the textured aran one. (28cms long after felting)

Turquoise bag	Colinette Banyan	approx 24cms square
Brown bag	Noro Kureyon	approx 25cms square
White bag	Colinette Lasso	approx 28cms square
Black bag	DK chenille	approx 30cms square
Cream bag	Aran yarn	approx 40cms square
Grey bag	Rowan Tapestry	approx 37cms square

---

[1] Nappies is the British Term for diapers

Once you've chosen your yarn (and a suitable hook), you need to decide on a stitch pattern. I used a basic stitch (dc), an openwork stitch, an all over pattern and a textured stitch, so virtually any stitch will work. When the square is folded to make the bag, the rows on the 2 sides of the front are at right angles to each other, and the rows on the back and flap run diagonally. This shows up more with some stitches. It is hard to tell on the openwork bag, but obvious on the double crochet bag. The popcorns on the textured square run diagonally and this continues when it is folded.

Having chosen your stitch pattern, simply make a chain the required length and work a square. If you're unsure of how many chain you need, either add on extra ones which can be undone later, or leave a long tail end so that extra chain can be worked if necessary. As a guide for the size of your square, the length of the finished bag will be approximately the same size as the length of one of the sides of the square. A quick way of checking if you've got a square is to fold a corner to it's diagonal opposite. When they meet and form a triangle, you've got a square.

If you will be using a loop and button fastening, you can make the chain loop before you fasten off.

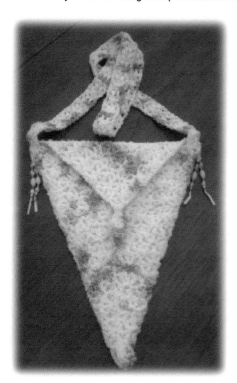

Embellishment.

If you want to embellish your bag, do it before you sew it up. On the black bag, I used a metallic slub yarn to work surface dc, and 5 other yarns to work surface ss over the square. I attached some dc rings (4 or 6 ch joined into a circle, then work dc over the circle) worked in metallic thread and finally on the flap I added some beads.

Linings

All of my bags are lined - except for the felted one - it is necessary for the openwork one, but it gives body to all of the bags. I hate sewing, so I've worked out a way of making the linings which is easy for me to do, but if you have a better way, please use it. I use lining material, and medium weight interfacing for extra stability if necessary.
To make the lining:

Choose a lining to match your yarn, but if you are working an openwork pattern you could use a contrast colour.

Lining with interfacing:

Use your square as a template and cut out a piece of interfacing. Cut 2 pieces of fabric, each approximately 1 cm bigger all round than the interfacing. Place the interfacing on top of one of the pieces of fabric, pin and fold the fabric overlap onto the interfacing. Place the second piece of fabric on top, fold the overlap to form a hem and pin in place, enclosing the interfacing. Catch stitch together.

Lining without interfacing:

I still use 2 pieces of fabric, folding a single 1cm hem all the way around, then stitching the 2 pieces together. If you use a single piece of lining, fold a double hem.

As an alternative, you can cut a piece of felt very slightly smaller than the crocheted square, and stitch it to the square. If you do this, attach the strap and fastening first so that they can be covered by the lining. (See Making up for information about attaching the strap).

Straps:

I have made a different strap for most of the bags, but you don't have to use these if you have other ideas.

Turquoise bag: Use a thin cotton (no 5 or no 3 cotton perle works well) to make a chain the length of the strap, then slip stitch back and fasten off.
 Use the main yarn to work dc over the slip stitch cord. This cord twists naturally, so I added a few more twists when I attached it.

Embellished bag: This strap is a 4 strand cord. Cut 4 lengths longer than the required finished length - you can always make the cord shorter - and tie them together at one end. Take the outside left strand under the next 2 strands to the right and back over the second of these strands (it is now the second strand from the left). Take the outside right strand under the next 2 strands to the left and back over the second of these strands (it is now the second strand on the right). Repeat these moves for the required length, then knot the cord at the bottom. For a thicker cord, you can chain the yarns first.

Brown bag: This has a simple slip stitch cord. Work a chain the required length, then slip stitch back again. Fasten off.

White bag: I used one repeat of the pattern plus an extra treble to make the strap and then threaded thin ribbon through the chain spaces. Stitch the ribbon in place before attaching the strap.

Cream bag: I wanted a thicker cord for this larger bag. First I cut a piece of piping cord the length I wanted the strap to be, then worked a 4 raised treble tube around it. To do this, make 6 chain, work 1 tr into the 4th ch from hook, 1 tr into each chain to end (4 tr). Fold in half and place the cord inside. Work a raised treble into each treble, in a spiral, until the cord is covered. Using sewing thread, stitch the ends of the piping cord to the crochet. This is another cord which spirals naturally.

Felted bag: This also has a slip stitch cord.

Fastenings:

I have used button and loop fastenings for all of the bags, 2 are commercial buttons, 2 are crochet covered button and 2 are needle felted i into a ball shaped button. To make covered buttons, you can use the same yarn as the bag, or a thinner (no. 5 or no. 8) cotton perle. Start off with 6 dc worked over a loop, slip stitch to first dc and tighten loop. On the next round, work 2 dc into each stitch, on the following round work 2 dc in every other stitch. Continue like this, working one more stitch between increases, until the circle is slightly smaller than the button. Now start to decrease on each round, working 1 stitch less between decreases until you have 6 dc again. Fasten off, leaving a long tail. Weave the tail through the stitches and gather up. Use the tail to sew on the button. For the needle felted buttons, I sewed a small loop on the back of the button before attaching it.

Making up:

Place the crochet square so that the corners face north, south, east and west. Fold the east and west corners to the centre and sew front seam. Do the same with the lining. If you want, you can sew across the bottom of the lining about 5 cms above the point.

Attach the strap to the bag. You can sew it to the inside of the bag or the outside of the lining.

Sew on button. Place the lining into the bag and stitch into place around the flap and across the front.

Stitch Sample Hat & Scarf

By Gail E. (Stitch'n'Frog) and Wendy G.(Ladybug's Crochet)

Note from the Big Cheese: This pattern can be made for both children and adults. Instructions indicate the sizes and materials used.

Adult Size Scarf

6 oz Worsted Weight 4-ply yarn for scarf & hat
I hook for Adult
H hook for Child
Needle to work ends in

Adult Size Scarf	Row 4: 1 tr in 2nd stitch and each st to end. Ch 4, turn.
Ch 21	Row 5: tr in 4th st, *ch 1, tr in first skipped stitch, skip 2 sts, tr in next stitch – repeat to end, ending with 1 tr in last st. Ch 1, turn.
Row 1: sc in 2nd chain from hook and in each stitch to end (21 sts) ch 2, turn. (20 stitches throughout)	Row 6: 1 sc in 1st st and each stitch across. Ch 1, turn.
Row 2: 1 hdc in first st and each st to end. Ch 2, turn.	Row 7: 1 BLO sc in each st across. Ch 1, turn.
Row 3: 1 dc in 2nd stitch and each st to end. Ch 3 turn.	Row 8: 1 FLO sc in each st across. Ch 2, turn.

Row 9: 1 hdc in first st and each st across, end with hdc in last st. Ch2, turn.

Row 8: *FP hdc in next st, BP hdc in next st – repeat across, ending with hdc in 2nd ch of turning chain. Ch 1, turn.

Row 10 & 11: *FP hdc in next st, BP hdc in next st – repeat across, ending with hdc in 2nd ch of turning chain. Ch 2, turn.

Row 12: *FP hdc in next st, BP hdc in next st – repeat across, ending with hdc in 2nd ch of turning chain. Ch 1, turn.

Row 13: sc in each st across. Ch 1, turn.

Row 14: 1 BLO sc in each st across. Ch 1, turn.

Row 15: 1 FLO sc in each st across. Ch 4, turn.

Row 16: tr in 4th st, *ch 1, tr in first skipped stitch, skip 2 sts, tr in next stitch – repeat to end, ending with 1 tr in last st. Ch 1, turn.

Repeat rows 13-16, 20 times, or until almost as long as you want the scarf.

For Ending of Scarf:

Row 1: sc in each st across. Ch 1, turn.

Row 2: 1 BLO sc in each st across. Ch 1, turn.

Row 3: 1 FLO sc in each st across. Ch 2, turn.

Row 4: 1 hdc in first st and each st to end. Ch 2, turn.
Row 5, 6, 7: *FP hdc in next st, BP hdc in next st – repeat across, ending with hdc in 2nd ch of turning chain. Ch 2, turn

Row 9: sc in each st across. Ch 1, turn.

Row 10: 1 BLO sc in each st across. Ch 1, turn.

Row 11: 1 FLO sc in each st across. Ch 4, turn.

Row 12: tr in 4th st, *ch 1, tr in first skipped stitch, skip 2 sts, tr in next stitch – repeat to end, ending with 1 tr in last st. Ch 1, turn.

Row 13: 1 sc in 1st st and each stitch across. Ch 4, turn.

Row 14: 1 tr in 2nd stitch and each st to end. Ch 2, turn

Row 15: 1 dc in 2nd stitch and each st to end. Ch 2 turn

Row 16: 1 hdc in first st and each st to end. Ch 1, turn.

.Row 17: 1 sc in 1st st and each stitch across.

End yarn. Add fringe to both ends, in each corner and every 3rd stitch across.

Child's Size Stitch Sampler Scarf

3 oz 3-ply/Sport Weight yarn for scarf & hat
H hook
Needle to work ends in
Ch 15
Row 1: sc in 2nd chain from hook and in each stitch to end (14 sts) ch 2, turn. (14 stitches throughout)
Work all rows the same as the adult scarf, when almost long enough to suit you, skip to Row 1 of Ending of Scarf.

Adult & Child Stitch Sampler Cap

Directions	Rnd 7: ch 1, sc in BLO of same stitch as join, sc in BLO of each st around. join with sl st in first sc.
Ch 5, join with sl st to form a ring.	Rnd 8: ch 2, *1 FP hdc in next stitch, 1 BP hdc in next st. repeat around, join with sl st in 2nd ch of starting chain.
Rnd 1: ch 3, make 13 dc in ring, join with sl st in 3rd ch of starting chain. (14 dc)	Rnds 9 & 10: repeat round 8, with FP in FP, and BP in BP, join with sl st in 2nd chain of starting chain.
Rnd 2: ch 3, 1 dc in same stitch as joining stitch, 2 dc in each stitch around, join with sl st in 3rd ch of starting chain. (28 dc)	Rnd 11: ch 1, sc in BLO of the same stitch as joining, and in each stitch around. join with sl st in 1st sc.
Rnd 3: ch 3, 1 dc in same stitch as join, dc in next stitch, *2 dc in next stitch, 1 dc in next stitch. Repeat around, join with sl st in 3rd ch of starting chain. (42 dc)	Rnd 12: ch 1, sc in FLO of same stitch as joining and each stitch around. join in 1st sc.
Rnd 4: ch 3, dc in same stitch as join, 1 dc in each of the next 2 stitches, *2 dc in next stitch, 1 dc in each of the next 2 stitches. repeat around. join with sl st in 3rd ch of starting chain. (56 stitches)	Rnd 13: ch 5 (counts as the first tr + 1sc) (mark the 4th ch to join at the end) now going backwards, skip 1 stitch and tr in the next one. Going forward again, *skip next 2 sts, tr in 3rd, ch 1, tr in the first missed stitch. repeat around, join with sl st in 4nd ch of starting chain.
Rnd 5: ch 2, hdc in same stitch, 1 hdc in next 3 stitches, *2 hdc in next stitch, 1 hdc in next 3 stitchs. repeat around, join with sl st in 2nd ch of starting chain. (70 sts from here forward)	Rnd 14: ch 1, sc in same stitch as join and each stitch around – with 1 sc between the "X" and 2 sc inside of the "X". join with sl st in first sc.
Rnd 6: ch 4, tr in each stitch around. Join with sl st in BLO in the 4th ch of starting chain.	Rnd 15: ch 1 sc in same st as join. 1 sc in each st around. Join with sl st in FLO of first sc. Rnd 16: ch 1, sc in FLO of same st as join. 1 sc in FLO of each st around. Join with sl st in first sc. End yarn, weave ends in.

Child's Stitch Sampler Cap

H hook for child
Needle for weaving ends

Directions	
Ch 5, join with sl st to form a ring.	**Rnd 10:** ch 1, sc in BLO same stitch as joining, and in of each stitch around. join in 1st sc in FOL.
Rnd 1: ch 3, make 13 dc in ring, join with sl st in 3rd ch of starting chain. (14 dc)	**Rnd 11:** ch 1, sc in FLO of same stitch as joining and each stitch around. join in 1st sc.
Rnd 2: ch 3, 1 dc in same stitch as joining stitch, 2 dc in each stitch around, join with sl st in 3rd ch of starting chain. (28 dc)	**Rnd 12:** ch 5 (counts as the first tr + 1sc) (mark the 4th ch to join at the end) now going backwards, skip 1 stitch and tr in the next one. Going forward again, *skip next 2 sts, tr in 3rd, ch 1, tr in the first missed stitch. repeat around, join with sl st in 4nd ch of starting chain.
Rnd 3: ch 3, 1 dc in same stitch as join, 1 dc in next stitch, *2 dc in next stitch, 1 dc in next stitch. Repeat around, join with sl st in 3rd ch of starting chain. (42 dc)	**Rnd 13:** ch 1, sc in same stitch as join and each stitch around – with 1 sc between the "X" and 2 sc inside of the "X". join with sl st in first sc.
Rnd 4: ch 2, hdc in same stitch as join, 1 hdc in next 2 stitches, *2 hdc in next stitch, 1 hdc in next 2 stitchs. repeat around, join with sl st in 2nd ch of starting chain. (56 sts from here forward)	**Rnd 14:** ch 1 sc in same st as join. 1 sc in each st around. Join with sl st in FLO of first sc.
Rnd 5: ch 4, tr in each stitch around. Join with sl st in BLO in 4th ch of starting chain	**Rnd 15:** ch 1, sc in FLO of same st as join. 1 sc in FLO of each st around. Join with sl st in first sc.
Rnd 6: ch 1, 1 sc in BLO of same stitch as join, hdc in BLO in each st around. join with sl st in first sc.	If desired, ch 1, 1 sc in same stitch as joining, 1 RSC in each stitch around. join, end yarn, weave ends in.
Rnd 7: ch 2, *1 FP hdc in next stitch, 1 BP hdc in next st. repeat around, join with sl st in 2nd ch of starting chain. **Rnds 8 & 9:** repeat round 7, with FP in FP, and BP is BP, join with sl st in 2nd chain of starting chain.	Follow the same hat pattern but change hooks & yarn~ For baby: Red Heart Jamie yarn (or any 3-ply baby yarn) 3-ply yarn F hook For older child - H hook and 3-ply yarn

Part III

Hook-a-look-a-ding-dong

There is no rhyme or reason to this book...it is a journey.

Are you having fun yet?

For some strange reason snob appeal has come into play in the fiber arts. I don't quite understand why. People like to make excuses that one craft was done by gentry and other crafts were done by peasants. Those may be historical facts, but in today's world those are not relevant facts.

We sit upon a cusp of change, where old forms of expression are quickly dying out as new, less complicated, and less thought provoking activities become the past times of choice (watching movies, and television, and yes...sniff..video games...(I sniff because I like video games!). We could lose our handcrafting and fiber art heritage as easily as we are losing species of animals in the rainforest, and what do we do? Do we rally round to save the old crafts for the future knowledge of humanity? (I mean, if all hell breaks loose SOMEONE needs to know how to sew on buttons!)

No, we bicker and crow over who is better, and who is to be lesser. I would hate to see the CLF help to move crochet out of the shadows and into the light to see we, the underdogs , soon become a wolf pack.

There is no one fiber art superior to any other. All fiber arts meet the needs and requirements of those who enjoy their craft(s).

 Let us not put down that which we do not understand. Let us not denigrate the patterns that do not make sense. Let us not do unto others as they have done unto us...Let's just rock the world with what we do best.

HOOK!

Does it really matter what other people say?

Can't you just be comfortable in your own skin?

Answers: a) Not really. b) Sure.

But isn't it nice to be treated with respect and kindness?

Veritas, Equitas

Fingerless gloves in crochet jacquard (back loop Tapestry Crochet).

By Danielle Krasner (aka Laracroft)

Skill Level: experienced in tapestry or jacquard crochet

Materials: Scraps of sock or fingering weight yarn: 4 greens in different shades, off-white, red, puce, one variegated multi-colour yarn
(Colinette Jitterbug "Toscana" used here).

Equipment: 2.5mm crochet hook.
2mm crochet hook.
Tapestry needle.
Two buttons or links

Gauge: 23 stitches x 22 rows = 3x3 inches in jacquard.

Stitches used: slip stitch (sl st), single crochet (sc), crochet jacquard (see Tutorial),
backwards crochet (see Tutorial).

Size: women's medium size.

Before you start:

Main section is worked from the top (fingers) down, in the round. Rounds are not joined but worked in a continuous spiral. The cuff is worked flat in rows, using backwards crochet on alternate rows to maintain stitch structure.

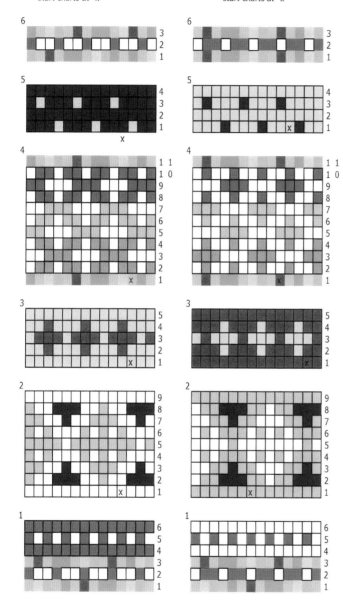

Fingers:

Using 2mm hook, ch 57. Join in a circle, being careful not to twist. (I use the smaller hook because my chains are always too loose. If your chains are always too tight, use the 2.5mm!)

Change to 2.5mm hook.

Work charts 1 and 2 in crochet jacquard across 57 sts.

Palm Band:

Working chart 3,

Rnd 1: sc2tog, continue in pattern (solid colour rnd) = 56 sts.
Rnd 2: in pattern
Rnd 3: in pattern
Rnd 4: in pattern.

For Right Glove:
Rnd 5: in background colour, ch 21, sk 6 sts, sc in 7th st. Place marker A in last sc before chain. Place marker B in sc just made. Cont in patt (solid colour rnd) to end of rnd. 50 palm sts + 21 ch = 71 sts.
For Left Glove:
Rnd 5: in patt (solid colour rnd) to 7th st before end of rnd. Ch 21, sk 6 sts, sc in last st of rnd. (Join variegated yarn on last loop) Place marker B in last sc before chain. Place marker A in sc just made. 50 palm sts + 21 ch = 71 sts.

<u>Palm/Thumb Gusset</u>:

Working chart 4,

Note: the pattern for the gusset differs slightly from the chart, but can't be charted! Therefore the gusset decreases will be explained row by row.

Right Glove: **(the gusset is shaped at the beginning of each row)**

Rnd 1: (one variegated strand): work 21 sc (blo) across chain. Work 50 sc around palm. Move markers up with each row. = 71 sts.

Rnd 2: 2sc G (green), 1sc W (white), continue in rnd2 of chart 4 as established, ending 2G. 22 gusset sts incl marker B + 49 palm sts incl marker A= 71 sts.

Rnd 3: sc1G, sc3W, sc3G, continue in chart 4 as established, ending 1G.
Rnd 4: Gusset: sc2togG, sc1 W, *sc2togG, sc1G, sc2togG, sc1W* 3 times. Sc1G in marked st. Palm: Sc 1G, 1W, 2G, 1W, 2G, continue in chart 4 as established, ending 2G. 15 gusset sts (incl marker B) + 49 palm sts (incl marker A) = 64 sts.

Rnd 5: (don't forget to change background colour!) Gusset: Sc1G, Sc2tog G, *sc1W, sc3G*, 3 times. Palm: sc3W, sc3G, continue in chart 4 as established until 2 sts before marker A. Sc2togG, sc1G in marked st. 14 gusset sts + 48 palm sts = 62 sts.

Rnd 6: Gusset: *sc1G, sc3W* 3 times, sc2togG. Palm: 1G, 1W, 2G, 1W, 2G, continue in chart 4 as established, ending 1G in st A. 13 gusset sts + 48 palm sts = 61 sts.

Rnd 7: Gusset: sc2togG, sc1W, *sc3G, sc1W* twice, sc2togG. Palm: sc3G, 3W, continue in chart 4 as established, ending 3W. 11 gusset sts + 48 palm sts = 59 sts.

Rnd 8: (2nd colour change!) Gusset: sc2togG, sc1G, sc1W, sc3G, sc1W, sc1G, sc2togG. Palm: sc1G, sc1W, sc2G, sc1W, continue in chart 4 as established. 9 gusset sts + 48 palm sts = 57 sts.
Rnd 9: Gusset: *sc1G, sc3W* twice, sc1G. Palm: Sc3W, sc3G, continue in chart4 as established. 9 gusset sts + 48 palm sts = 57 sts.

Rnd 10: Gusset: sc2togG, sc1W, sc1G, sc2togG, sc1W, sc2togG. Palm: sc1G, sc1W, sc2G, sc1W, Cont in chart 4 as established, sc last 2 sts tog. 6 gusset sts + 47 palm sts = 53 sts.

Rnd 11: sc 53 in variegated yarn. Join round and bind off.

Left Glove: **(The gusset is shaped at the end of each row)**

Rnd 1: (one variegated strand): Work 50 sc around palm. Work 21 sc (blo) across chain. Change to new colour at marked st A. Move markers up with each row. = 71 sts.

Rnd 2: Starting at marker A, 2sc W, 1sc G, continue in chart 4 as established, ending 2W. 49 palm sts incl. marker A + 22 gusset sts including marker B

Rnd 3: Sc1W in marked st, sc3G, sc3W, continue in chart 4 as established, ending 1W

Rnd 4: Palm: Starting at marker A, sc2W, 1G, continue in chart 4 as established until marker B. Gusset: In marked st B, sc1W. Sc1G, *sc2togW, sc1W, sc2togW, sc1G* 3 times, sc2togW. 49 palm sts incl st A + 15 gusset sts incl st B = 64 sts

Rnd 5: Palm: (Change pattern colour!) Sc1W in st A. Sc3W, sc3G, continue in chart 4 as established until marker B. Gusset: starting at st B, *sc3W, sc1G* 3 times, sc1W, sc2togW. 49 palm sts incl st A + 14 gusset sts incl st B = 63 sts.

Rnd 6: Palm: sc2togW over st A and next st, replace marker in st just made. sc1G, sc2W, continue in chart 4 as established until marker B. Gusset: Starting at st B, sc2togW (replace marker in st just made), *sc3G, sc1W* 3 times. 48 palm sts incl st A + 13 gusset sts incl st B = 61 sts.

Rnd 7: Palm: Starting in st A, sc3G, sc3W, continue in chart 4 as established until marker B. Gusset: sc2togW over st B and next st, replace marker in st just made. *Sc1G, sc3W* twice, sc1G, sc2W. 48 palm sts + 12 gusset sts = 60 sts.

Rnd 8: Palm: (2nd colour change!) sc1W in st A, sc1G, sc2W, sc1G, continue in chart 4 as established until marker B. Gusset: sc1W in st B, sc2togW, sc1G, sc3W, sc1G, sc2W, sc2togW. 48 palm sts + 10 gusset sts = 58 sts.

Rnd 9: Palm: starting at st A, sc3W, sc3G. continue in chart 4 as established until marker B. Gusset: sc1W in st B. Sc3G, sc1W, sc3W, sc2togW. 48 palm sts + 9 gusset sts = 57 sts.

Rnd 10: Palm: Sc1W in A, sc2togW, sc1W, sc1G, sc2W , continue in chart 4 as established until marker B. Gusset: sc2togW over st B and next st, sc1G, sc1W, sc2togW, sc1G, sc2togW, join on variegated yarn. 47 palm sts + 6 gusset sts = 53 sts.

Rnd 11: sc 53 in variegated yarn. Join round and bind off.

<u>Wrist:</u>

Right Glove: Join yarn in 7th st before end of last rnd (not incl the joining sl st.)

Left Glove: Join yarn in 7th st after end of last rnd (not incl the joining sl st.)

Row 1: ch1, sc in BLO around = 52 sts. Ch1, turn.

Row 2: work in backwards crochet FLO to end. Ch1, turn.

Row 3: working in crochet jacquard (BLO), work row 1 of chart 5. Ch1, turn.

Row 4: working in backwards crochet FLO, work row 2 of chart 5.
        Carry the unused thread back as you go, but pick it up only when you work into the pattern sts, leaving "floats".
Ch1, turn.

Row 5: in jacquard, work row 3 of chart 5. You can weave in the "floats" as you work this row. Ch1, turn.
Row 6-17: sc across in background colour.

Trim:

Weave in any ends on the wrist section before starting trim.

Rnd 1: Join variegated yarn in 1st st of last row. Sc around. Sc 3 into last st, then continue up right selvedge, picking up sts evenly. Continue down left selvedge, ending in side of 1st st.

Rnd2: Join white in 1st st. Continue in chart 6 around. Work 3sc in center st of 3sc of previous row. Continue up right edge to upper point of wrist opening, sk 1, continue down left edge , ending in side of 1st st.

Rnd 3: Join variegated yarn in 1st st. Sc around. Work 4 sc in center st of 3sc of previous row. Continue up right edge to upper point of wrist opening, sk1. Measure for button placement. Continue down left edge, making buttonhole where desired by working ch2 (ch3, or ch4, depending on the size of your button!) sk2(or however many chs made) sc to end of opening. Sl st in 1st st of row. Bind off.

<u>Thumb:</u>

Working chart 3,
Rnds 1-5: Pick up 27 + 1 sts around thumb opening. Work chart 3 in rounds across 28 sts.

Rnd 6: Sc around in variegated yarn. Sl st to join, bind off.

Tutorial 1: Crochet Jacquard

By Danielle Krasner (laracroft)

1. Hold strand A in the normal way, and strand B just over the working edge.

2. Insert hook and pass under B to pick up A.

3. Pull A through.
To continue in A, pull A through both loops on hook and repeat from step 1.

4. To change colours, pass the hook behind A and pick up B.

4.   Pull B through both loops, completing the stitch.

5.   Insert hook, pick up B and pull it through..

6.Complete the stitch with A if your next stitch is in A. If you need to do another stitch in B, then repeat from step 4. To continue with several stitches in B, change the position of the two strands so that B is held normally.

TUTORIAL 2: Backwards crochet

1.   With wrong side facing you, insert the hook from back to front towards you, into the front loop only. (if you were looking at the right side, that would be the back loop.)

2.   Swing your hook up to catch the working strand from above, turning the hook down counterclockwise to pick it up.

3.   And pull it through to the back.

4.   Twist the hook clockwise to pick up the last loop, and pull it through.

For the cuff section of "Veritas, Equitas", you won't need to work stitches in two colours when working backwards, but you will need to pick up the floating thread as you go. Like this:

1. Hold the float in front of the work. Insert hook as before.

2. Catch the float, then grab A (yellow here) by twisting the hook counterclockwise.

3. Pull A through to the back, then twist clockwise to pull up a loop and draw through.

A Hook can show Love

(and stop anyone, even me from drinking)
By Danielle Angelo (Aka Dani)

I am a mom, a military wife, a friend and I come armed with a hook. A hook that brought me comfort and love. In early 2004 my husband came home one day with the dreaded news, he was being deployed to Iraq. Now we are not one of those families who thought "this won't happen to his unit", we knew full well that this is just one of those things that can happen within a blink of an eye being a reserve military family.

Of course one of the first things that went through my mind was the craziness that was Iraq at the time. But as we prepared for his upcoming departure my mind then moved to what am I going to do with myself in the evenings? My husband and I of 16 years at the time really enjoy spending time together in the evenings. It's our wind down time, our time together after our two girls are tucked so sweetly (told for the third time I'm sure that its lights out time) in bed. I figured I could surf the net, read a book or fold laundry just so many nights alone before I turned to alcoholic drinks in some form or another.

A couple weeks after he left, the girls and I were next door at our charming neighbor's (Harriett) house. The girls were swimming while Harriett and I chatted.   It was a warm lovely day so Harriett asked if we could move back into her house because she was working on a craft project for her woman's group. I asked what she was working on; she said it was called a lapghan. I had no idea the can of worms I was opening with my next question "what's a lapghan?"

Harriett then showed me what I now know to be a Rectangle Granny Square Afghan, her woman's group made them for retirement & convalescent homes for people who were confined to wheel chairs. The rectangle shape allowed those who needed them to cover their legs without adding tons of bulk on the sides or over flow of the afghan to get caught up in the wheels. I loved the colors she was using, the shape and the ease in which she created the stitches. She grabbed another hook, started the center part of a granny square and then showed me the crochet double stitch.

That was my first afghan; I ended up giving it to Harriett for her woman's group. I ran right out, bought several hooks, a couple skeins of yarn and a beginner crochet book. I wish I could sit here and say I was off running, the only thing I did was run smack into a brick wall in regards to printed instructions and those lovely illustrations. If I thought I loved the world wide web before it now became the light of hope in my crochet world after finding www.stitchguide.com. One video after another showing me stitch after stitch, I started to think that I could in fact conquer hook and yarn.

My husband was deployed for eight months; in that time I managed to learn was a few new things such as YAS, yarn acquisition syndrome. PAS, pattern acquisition syndrome. I learned just how many crochet magazines and books one can place around the house in pretty wicker baskets. I also learned that yarn can be stored nearly anywhere within ones home... baskets, shelves, Rubbermaid containers, closets, glove boxes in the family mini van and even in the entertainment center next to your DVD player.

As the time of his deployment passed I learned that the evenings passed in chunks of time consisting of 4 afghans, way too many to count scarves, hats & hair scrunchies, and 4 ponchos. Before I knew it Joe was home. We are now near the end of our family's second deployment and the hook has now not only shown me love but I've been able to pass the love on to my oldest daughter.

I will always be grateful for Harriett sharing her love of yarn and hook. So remember the next time someone sees you crocheting and asks, "what are you doing?" Tell them to grab a hook & yarn and teach them the love of crochet.

We join our hero on the quest to summit...

By Karen Kesecker

To be continued...

This creature was inspired by a novelty song I learned in my childhood. It was a popular song written by Sheb Wooley about a 'one-eyed, one-horned ,flying purple people eater' who comes to Earth to join a rock and roll band!

The song hit the charts in 1958, and over the years there has been much speculation about whether the creature himself was purple, or whether the people he ate were purple.

For me, he is a purple creature... but you should feel free to let your imagination guide you on this one!

~ Sharon Maher – Laughing Purple Goldfish Designs (aka Laughingpurple)

purple people eater

Photo by Sharon Maher

Materials:

Hook: 3.0 mm

Yarn: DK weight yarn of your choice:
     Small amounts of white, black, green, red
     Medium amount of purple

Stuffing

Yarn needle

Gauge: Ensure your tension is tight enough to make a firm fabric so stuffing does not peek out.

US crochet terms used throughout.

Part 1: Begin Body Use purple yarn to make a magic adjustable loop	
Round 1	Work 8sc into ring, then tighten
Round 2	Inc. in every stitch (16)
Round 3	Inc. in every 2nd stitch (24)
Round 4	Inc. in every 3rd stitch (32)
Round 5	Inc. in every 4th stitch (40)
Round 6	Inc. in every 5th stitch (48)
Round 7	Inc. in every 6th stitch (56)
Round 8	Inc. in every 7th stitch (64)
Rounds 9 to 19	Sc in every stitch (64) For 11 rows
Round 20	Dec. in every 7th stitch (56)
Round 21	• Sc in every stitch (56)
Round 22	• Dec. in every 6th stitch (48)
Round 23	• Sc in every stitch (48)
Round 24	• Dec. in every 5th stitch (40)
Round 25	• Sc in every stitch (40)
Round 26	Dec. in every 4th stitch (32)
Round 27	Dec. in every 3rd stitch (24)
Round 28	Dec. in every 2nd stitch (16)
Round 29	Dec. in every stitch (8)
Stuffs Before you go any further	
Round 30	Dec. in every stitch (4)

Part 2: Begin Eyeball	
Use black yarn to make a magic adjustable loop	
Round 1	Work 8 sc into ring, then tighten
Round 2	Inc. in every stitch (16)
Change To white yarn	
Round 3	Inc. in every 2nd stitch (24)
Rounds 4, 5 & 6	Sc in every stitch (24)
Round 7	Dec. in every 2nd stitch (16)
Round 8	Dec. in every stitch (8)
Stuff Before you go any further	
Round 9	Dec. in every stitch (4)
Cut yarn Use the tail to sew small opening closed	

Part 3: Begin Eyelid	Use purple yarn to ch11
Round 1	Skip 1st chain then sc into next 10, turn work upside down and work sc into the other side of each chain (you should now be back where you started) (22)
Round 2	Work 10sc, inc. in next stitch. Repeat (24)
Round 3	Work 11sc, inc. in next stitch. Repeat (26)
Round 4	Work 12sc, inc. in next stitch. Repeat (28)
Round 5	Work 13sc, inc. in next stitch. Repeat (30)
Rounds 6 & 7	Sc in every stitch (30)
Cut yarn Sew in ends	
Position eye	Inside the eyelid and stitch firmly in place
Whip stitch	Around edge of eyelid as illustrated, using green yarn and yarn needle

Begin Wings (make 2) Use green yarn to make a magic adjustable ring	
Row 1	Work 3dc into ring
Row 2	Inc. in 1st stitch, dc, inc. in last stitch (5)
Row 3	Inc. in 1st stitch, 3dc, inc. in last stitch (7)
Row 4	Inc. in 1st stitch, 5dc, inc. in last stitch (9)
Rows 5, 6 & 7	Dc in every stitch (9)
Cut yarn Leave enough length to attach to body later	

Edging

Use green to sc along the sides of the wings, work 3sc at the tip

changeTo purple yarn and sc into each stitch along the edging, work 3sc at the tip again

Whip stitch

Around edge of wing as illustrated, using white yarn and wool needle

Part: 5 **Begin Horn** Use white yarn to make a magic adjustable loop	
Round 1	Work 4sc into loop, tighten
Round 2	Sc into every stitch (4)
Round 3	Inc. in every 2nd stitch (6)
Rounds 4 to 8	Sc into every stitch (6)For 5 rounds
Round 9	Inc. in every 2nd stitch (9)
Rounds 10 to 14	Sc into every stitch (9) For 5 rounds
Round 15	Inc. in every 3rd stitch (12)
Rounds 16 to 18	Sc into every stitch (12)For 3 rounds

Cut yarn Leaving approx 45cm long tail

Stuff Leaving bottom open

Create curve

Thread needle with the tail of yarn attached to your work. Make a running stitch in a straight line up to the tip of the horn. Pull yarn tightly, which will bend the horn across to one side. Make a few small stitches to secure, then run the yarn back down to the base of the horn again and secure there. Leave yarn attached. You will use this tail to join the horn to the body.

Assembly: *Position eye, horn and wings to the body as seen in photo. Sew firmly in place.*

Use red yarn to stitch a zigzag shape for the mouth.

Behold the Power of the Swatch

by Tracie Barrett (traciecrochets)

I used to fear the swatch. I saw it as a waste of time, a waste of yarn, and a PIA. Granted, at the time, I was making afghans and swatches really aren't important, right? Wrong. But I'll get to that in a minute. I learned the hard way when I made a hat that would fit a baby doll that swatching might maybe be important.

Lately (in the past year) I've been a strong proponent of a swatch. Not just for checking gauge, although that's the most important point of it. Anytime anyone in our crochet group would ask, "Will this yarn work for this project?" the first word out of my mouth was "Swatch".

I was lucky enough in 2007 to take a class with Lily Chin. Now, I had read her take on swatching in her book. And I agreed with it and was starting to go by it. So in her class she gave all the reasons for swatching. And the main mantra was:

DO UNTO THE SWATCH WHAT YOU WILL DO UNTO THE FINAL ITEM

What does this mean? Let me post some of the questions I've seen on various forums and email lists (paraphrased) and show what swatching will do to answer the question.

1. I washed this item and it fell apart/colors ran/it felted/etc! What do I do?

Well, nothing now. Had you made a swatch (not just a 1" x 1", I'm talking a nice 6" x 6" swatch) and washed it how you planned on washing the item, then you'd know that you can't wash it on regular speed in hot water and dry it in the dryer. I'd rather waste a few yards of yarn and find out that I shouldn't toss that very detailed (and time consuming to make) sweater in with the rest of the laundry.

2. I have this yarn and want to use it for this project but it's not the yarn called for. Will it work?

SWATCH it! That's how you determine if going up three hook sizes will make a difference. Sure, you can hit gauge that way, but is it now so open in the stitch pattern that your sweater is nearly see-through? Or did you have to go down three hook sizes and now it's like wearing cardboard? Does the stitch pattern even show up in that yarn? Is it something you'd want to wear? SWATCH!!!!!!!!!

3. Will this yarn soften after I make a garment I want to wear next to my skin?

Make a swatch, wash it if you can, and spend the day with it pinned inside your shirt, sock, pants, wherever you're going to wear it. You'll know really quick if you can stand it or not. Better to have a reaction, reach in and pull the swatch out, then to be stuck out at a nice dinner and spend the whole evening wanting to rip the sweater off. While you'll make a whole new set of friends, you might not be able to eat there anymore.

4. Will this synthetic yarn block if I make a lacy design in it?

Swatch it and see. Spend the fifteen minutes making a mini version and find out that no, it won't block than spend thirty hours and find that out. Try wet blocking first, and if that doesn't work then try steam blocking. You may be surprised at just how many yarns will block. You'll also find in the swatching if the yarn wants you to go up or down a hook size.

5. Do you think this stitch pattern will work with this yarn?

Swatch it and see. Some stitch patterns are what Lily called "trophy wives": pretty to look at but a b*tch to live with. Find out in a 6" x 6" swatch that you hate that stitch pattern than two weeks later and half way through the project with the deadline looming.

6. Do these colors work / will they run / etc / etc?

Can you all answer this now? Swatch it, wash it, and see. I'd rather see on a swatch that the pretty red and white stripes become a pink mess than finish the sweater/blanket/purse and find that out.

7. Will this afghan I'm making out of acrylic soften up?
Actually, yes. I've softened up acrylic by washing on GENTLE cycle in cold water with a smidge of detergent and a full load's worth of softener. Also....you can steam block acrylic and it will totally change. Seriously, try it. Take the ickiest yarn you've got, make two swatches. Take one swatch and steam the daylights out of it under your iron (don't touch the iron to it, just hover). You will be amazed. I was. Don't hate the acrylic. It all has its place.

8. Do I have enough yarn to make this?

Swatch. Seriously. Do a good sized swatch (you can pull it back out if you have to if you need the yarn) and measure it. Measure the area of the item you're making (if its a garment, then measure each piece and figure the area and then add that up). Weigh your swatch. Now you have to do math. Let's use an example to make this make sense. Your swatch is 1/10th the area of your final piece. Your swatch weighs 3g. You will need about 30g to make your final piece. Make sense? If not, well, I'm not sure how much I can help you. It's math and I'm still struggling with it.

9. How much will this piece felt?

For the love of all that's yarny, SWATCH it and see! If it's something that requires a specific amount of felting, you better be doing swatches and felting them. This is also where you can see if different colors felt at different rates or if the colors run. Better here than later when it's done.

10. If I use this hook and this yarn can I size this project up or down?

SWATCH it. Again, this is how you can tell if it'll be too open or too tight, if it will even work, and how difficult it's going to be.

Now, I'm just as swamped on things as the next crocheter. But, I'd rather spend twenty minutes making a swatch to find out that my idea won't work than to spend three weeks or more on a project and have it come out like crap. So please, help yourself and do a swatch. You'll be amazed at how many questions you can answer yourself without having to frustrate others.

Examples of swatches:

Left: Basketweave swatch in handspun singles with commercial sock yarn. This swatch. Photo courtesy of Laurie Wheeler

Right: Broomstick lace swatch by

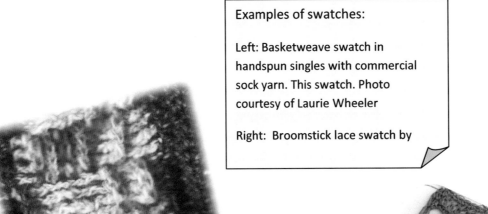

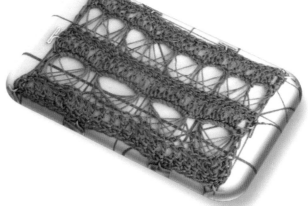

Yin Yang ball Keychain

By Mimi Alelis (aka MimiCat)

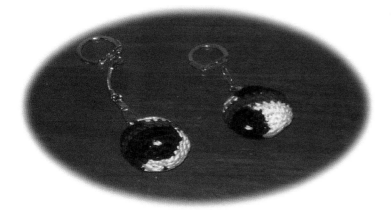

Skill: Intermediate

Materials: Cotton thread size 8 or size 10 (2 strands worked together): small amount white, small amount black, small amount red (or any contrasting color)

3.5mm steel hook.

Note: Other thread or yarn may be substituted. Gauge is not important.

Other materials: Plastic pellets or polyester fiberfill, metal keychain ring

Stitches/abbreviations used: ch - chain st , sc - single crochet, ss - slip st

Sc 2 tog – (draw a loop on the next st) twice, yo and draw through 3 loops

on hook

Changing colors: on the last sc before changing color, draw a loop on the next st, drop the previous color, yo with the succeeding color and draw up the two loops to finish the previous sc. Sc over the unused thread at the back of the work as you go along.

Instructions: (Note: The pattern is worked in continuous sc rounds.)

Rnd 1: Starting with white (W),ch 2, 3 sc in 2nd ch from hook , change to black (B), 3 sc in the same space (mark the beginning of rounds)

Rnd 2: with W, 2 sc in each of the next 3 sc, sc in next sc, change to B, sc in the same sc, 2 sc in next 2 sc (12 sc)

Rnd 3: with W, sc in the next 3 sc, change to B, sc in the same sc, change to W, sc in the next 2 sc, 2 sc in the next sc, sc in the next sc, change to B, sc in the next sc, 2 sc in the next sc, change to W sc in the next sc, change to B, sc in next sc, 2 sc in the next sc (16 sc)

Rnd 4: 2 sc in the next sc, change to W, 2 sc in the next sc, sc in the next 2 sc, 2 sc in each of the next 2 sc, sc in the next 2 sc, 2 sc in the next sc, sc in the next sc, change to B, sc in the same sc, sc in the next 2 sc, 2 sc in each of the next 2 sc, sc in the next 2 sc (24 sc)

Rnd 5: (continue with B), sc in each of the next 4 sc, change to W sc in the next 12 sc, change to B, sc in the next 8 sc (24 sc)

Rnd 6: sc in next 4 sc, change to red (R) sc in the next 20 sc (24 sc)

Rnd 7: (continue with R), sc in next 20 sc, change to B, sc in the next 4 sc (24 sc)

Rnd 8: (continue with B), sc in next 8 sc, change to W, sc in the next 12 sc, change to B, sc in the next 4 sc (24 sc)

Rnd 9: (continue with B), sc in next 9 sc, change to W, sc in the next 13 sc, change to B, sc in next 2 sc (24 sc)

Rnd 10: (continue with **B**), sc in next 2sc, sc next 2 tog, change to **W**, sc next 2 tog, change to **B**, sc in next 2 sc, sc 2 tog, change to **W**, sc 2 tog, sc in next 2 sc, sc next 2 tog twice, change to **B**, sc in next sc, change to **W**, sc in next sc, sc next 2 tog twice (16sc)

Rnd 11: Change to **B**, sc 2 tog, sc in next 2 sc, sc 2 tog, sc in next sc, change to **W**, sc in next sc, sc 2 tog, sc in next 2 sc, sc 2 tog, sc in next 2 sc (12 sc

Fill the mini ball with plastic pellets, and continue stuffing it as you finish the last round.

Rnd 12: change to **B**, sc 2 tog 3 times, change to **W**, sc 2 tog, 3 times (6 sc), join with ss. Ch 5 (loop) and fasten off, leaving 12 inches for sewing. Sew the loop in place and sew up the remaining 6 st. to close. Sew any remaining gaps

Finish project by connecting the metal ring of the keychain attachment with a long-nose pliers to finish the keychain.

Color Chart

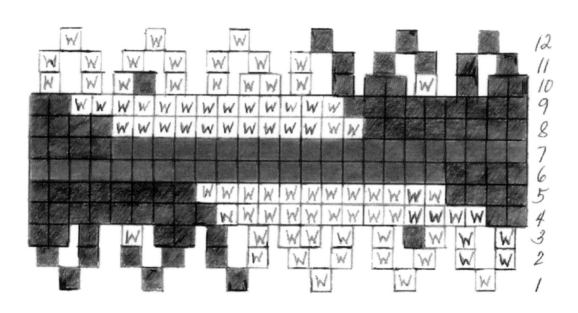

12
11
10
9
8
7
6
5
4
3
2
1

W - White   ■ - Black   ■ - Red

Dear CLF friends, it had been my intention to have the Secrets of Yarn Project: Crochet Edition finished and published before the CLF Book. We all know about intentions right? It's still in production at the time of this writing, but I felt this sample chapter might be of great use to crochet compatriots everywhere!

This is but a single chapter in a lengthy book that is dedicated to the women and men who use hooks and yarn to create wonderful things and warm memories for themselves and others!

~ Laurie A. Wheeler, CLF Founder and Fearless Leader

The Secrets of Yarn: Crochet Edition Chapter Seven
By Laurie A. Wheeler

The Key to unlocking yarn substitutions

Many times there is a pattern that is delicious, but for whatever reason you don't want or can't use the yarn listed in the pattern. Regardless of the reasons behind you wanting or needing to substitute the yarn, knowing how will make your life and projects much easier.

Let's look into the factors that make a good substitution (or planning any project for that matter!).

1) What kind of article is it?

2) What yarn is listed? (Brand/Weight)

3) How much yardage is listed (if any)

4) What is the original yarn made of (fiber), and what are acceptable substitutions?*

5) What is the gauge in the pattern?

*especially important in considering how the fabric will function, and dealing with sensitivities and possible allergic reactions by recipients of item.

1)   What kind of article is it?

This is the most important question to ask, every kind of object has a different set of needs in a yarn. A sweater needs to have stretch memory, wear-ability, and flexibility. A sock monkey needs to be firm, and washable. A vase has to be able to stand up or at least hold three dimensional shape. Socks ideally should not be too saggy or droopy in the cuffs, neither should they be too thick or scratchy. Baby blankets (in general) should be soft, and washable.

Considering the item itself will help in picking out a yarn to substitute for the one called in the pattern.

For example, I recently saw a men's vest pattern that I really want to make for my husband. I can use the yarn called for in the pattern, but truthfully the only time my husband wears, jackets or vests is when it is below freezing (yup, he's one of those), so acrylic won't really cut it. He'd prefer wool. I don't want to use my hand spun because he has a 56 in chest, his shoulders are wider than average, and so is his waist line. I will have to use the pattern as a guide, but really tweak it since it's measurements don't go as large as his do!

So, I know that this vest is going to be worn outside, and it will be worked in, hubby will be doing things like chain sawing downed trees, and walking in the woods. This vest will get worn often, by someone who works very hard, and likes to be out of doors.

2)   What yarn is listed?

If it is a yarn you know well, then it will be easier for you to make a substitution. You will already know how it works up, it's drape, stretch memory, and you may even have a swatch or two laying around a work basket! However, more and more yarns come out each year, and it could very well be a yarn that isn't easy to find at a nearby store, or it could be made out of a material you don't want to use.

If you do not know anything about the yarn, look it up online at yarndex.com. They list almost every yarn in the market. Now, their information is catering really to the knitting world, but you will find how many wraps per inch, or at least it's weight as defined by the Craft Yarn Council of America. That will begin to put you in the ball park.

Back to the example:

I will not list the yarn in the pattern I like, because I don't want people to think it's the yarn itself I don't like. Let's just say I like that yarn but not for this particular project. Already we have seen what needs are present in the project. The one thing the yarn in the pattern has going for it is that it is washable! Knowing I want to use wool, but need the garment to not shrink, my best bet is a super wash wool, or a wool/acrylic blend. There are several brands that make that kind of yarn that I find passable for this project (and once again, I really don't want or have time to spin that much yardage for this particular vest).

This will not be an heirloom piece (any more than the original design is meant to be), so I have no problem buying less expensive craft yarn.

I know this yarn's weight is about an Aran or worsted. So I need to find a comparable weight yarn. (My mind is already walking down the aisle at the craft store.)

3) How much yardage is listed?

If the pattern calls for four balls of yarn, each ball being 250 yds, the total project will take up to 1000 yards of yarn. Each company, and brand has different yardage amounts. More and more companies are putting the yardage on their labels. Make sure you know how much you will need for your project and then get one extra skein if you can! Why one extra? It's my general rule for just in case you make a mistake, or the cats find the last skein. Sometimes measurements are off, sometimes our gauge runs differently, or even more fun, sometimes we end up wanting to make a matching hat to go with the project! (Maybe not to match the afghan, but hey,you never know!)

For example:

The vest is going to require copious amounts of yardage. The pattern only goes up to X-Large, I am going to have to increase the pattern (we'll see how closely it resembles the original when I'm done, however my goal is that it fits my hubby), so I know that each skein of the yarn called for in the pattern is about 250 yds. It calls for four (4) skeins for X-Large. My bet is that would leave me short, I think really to be safe if I were using the yarn in the pattern I would have to use about five and a half skeins (maybe a full six, he has really really wide shoulders!) I'm looking at about 1500 yds, enough to make me a nice over sized sweater, I am quite grateful he prefers no sleeves.)

4) What is the original yarn made of and what are acceptable substitutions?

This is quite important. If the original yarn is made out of something that has a lot of drape, you don't want to substitute with a yarn that is bouncy and springy. I would not substitute linen with wool to put it simply. I might substitute with a linen blend, or a cotton/ poly blend, Manmade fibers may also provide the right mix of drape, sheen, and feel for this substitution. I wouldn't substitute wool with alpaca unless it was a blend, or if the original wool was Merino. I would substitute cotton and ingeo, polyester or nylon for silk (if the polyester/nylon had silk like qualities).Now that I've just confused the heck out of most people, I will put it in very simple terms: **Remember to use the table about fiber properties to see which things may play around well together**!

If you have allergies or issues of conscience, try to match the material as closely as possible, consider texture, integrity, stretch memory, etc. Remember that swatching is your friend!. This may be a case for acquiring some yarn samples and trying it out, or just buying one skein to see how it works up.

For example: The vest original pattern called for an acrylic yarn. Now this particular acrylic is actually passable in my book, it's not scratchy and works up beautifully. But, I know hubby will get more out of a wool or wool blend. We live in the Pacific Northwest and that means rain, the only fiber that will keep you warm when wet is wool. Other fibers keep out the rain (like mohair and cashmere) but good ol' wool actually retains heat even when it is soaked through.

100% wool, unless it is super wash, is a foolish thought for this project. To put it simply my husband does his own laundry. I really don't want to make this humongous vest only to have him felt and full it in the machine. In fact, I would probably cry if that were to happen, so to preserve the life of the vest, my husband and my marriage. I will most likely use a craft yarn that is mostly acrylic with some wool. (If it were for me? I'd go 100% handspun, but I would only need half the yarn for my vest!)

5) What is the gauge called for in the pattern?

This is your final check for yarn size. If the gauge is using an F hook, and it's: 15 stitches and 10 rows equals 3 inches, you are going to have a fairly good idea of what size yarn you will need. CAVEAT!!! Give yourself some wiggle room on the gauge, you may have different tension, find a yarn that will do that gauge with the hook size that will meet it. Often for me to reach a gauge listed in a pattern I have to go up a hook size, other people sometimes have to go down a hook (it also depends on what kind/brand of hook is used too!).

In summary, I wish I could give you one sure fire trick to make yarn substitutions easy and frustration free process. There is still a great amount of trial and error involved, but rest assured that the more you do it, the more knowledgeable and the easier it will be in the future. It's much easier for me to substitute yarns in my head now that I've actually learned about yarn, and crocheted more swatches than I have finished articles, than it was twenty years ago when I stuck to what I knew best.

WPI= Wraps Per Inch

This is the most accurate way to measure a yarn's size or weight. It's a term used in hand spinning and weaving, but really is the most uniform way to measure yarn by width. To measure yarn; take an item, such as a ruler, and wrap the yarn around it (not packing it super tightly, but close together) in a on e inch unit. Count the wraps, this will give you the WPI. A fine yarn has more WPI and Bulky has less.

SeaHorsin' Around

By Jennifer Reeve (aka Craftkitten)

Materials: Approximately 12 yards any weight yarn and hook 1 size smaller than yarn's suggested gauge or whatever size will make a tight enough fabric and not have holes that allow for stuffing leakage. Polyfil for stuffing. Small amount of sparkly fabric for fins (Optional). Small amount of black yarn for eyes or beads.

Sample 1 was made with Filatura di Crosa "Brilla".(120yds per ball sport weight 42% cotton 58% Rayon) and a Size E hook.

Sample 2 was made with Berroco "Cotton Twist" and a size F hook.

Sample 1 Finished dimensions: 6" from nose to tail
Gauge: 6sts & 6 rounds per inch

Sample 2 Finished dimensions: 7" from nose to tail Gauge: 5 sts & 5 ½ rounds per inch

Note: This is worked in 2 pieces. The Body is worked from tail to neck and the Head is worked from the neck ruff to the nose. Stuff with polyfil as you go.

Row 1	Sk first ch, 3sc in each of next 9 ch, 7sc in last ch (Fan made).	**34 sts**
Round 2	Begin working in round, 7scfan is beginning of round. Work 1 sc in first sc of 7scfan, work 1 sc in each of the fan.	7 sts
Rounds 3 & 4	Work even.	7 sts
Round 5	2sc in first sc, 1 in each sc of last 6 sc.	8 sts
Round 6	1sc in each of next 2 sc, 2sc in next sc, 1 in each of last 5sc.	9 sts
Round 7	1sc in each of next 4 sc, 2sc in next sc, 1 in each of last 4sc.	10 sts
Round 8	1sc in each of next 6 sc, 2sc in next sc, 1 in each of last 3sc.	11 sts
Round 9	1sc in each of next 5 sc, 2sc in next sc, 1 in each of last 5sc.	12 sts
Round 10	1sc in each of next 6 sc, 2sc in next sc, 1 in each of last 5sc.	13 sts
Round 11	1sc in each of next 7 sc, 2sc in next sc, 1 in each of last 5sc.	14 sts

Tail: Chain 11

Tummy		
Round 12	2sc in each of next 2 sc, 1 in each sc to last 3, 2 in each of last 3 sc.	19 sts
Round 13	2sc in each of next 2 sc, 1 in each sc to last 3, 2 in each of last 3 sc.	24 sts
Rounds 14-20	Work Even.	24 sts
Round 21	Sc2tog, 1 sc in each of next 20 sc, sc2tog in last 2 sc.	22 sts
Round 22	Sc2tog, 1 sc in each of next 18 sc, sc2tog in last 2 sc.	20 sts
Round 23	Sc2tog, 1 sc in each of next 16 sc, sc2tog in last 2 sc.	18 sts
Round 24	Sc2tog, 1 sc in each of next 14 sc, sc2tog in last 2 sc.	16 sts
Round 25	Sc2tog, 1 sc in each of next 12 sc, sc2tog in last 2 sc.	14 sts
Round 26	Sc2tog, 1 sc in each of next 10 sc, sc2tog in last 2 sc.	12 sts
Round 27	Work even.	12 sts

COLOR TWIST HAT

Designed by Nancy Smith Missyboo)

Textured bands on either side of the color twist center give visual appeal to this hat that's fun to make, and to wear. Fits average adult head (21"-23").

LEVEL: Easy for those who have changed colors in a project before...

MATERIAL:

Lion Brand CottonEase, 3.5oz/100g, 207yd/188m;

50% cotton, 50% acrylic;

16 sc + 17 rows = 4 inches (10 cm) with size G-6 (4 mm) hook

 1 skein Almond (#099) Color A

 1 skein Terracotta (#134) Color B

 1 skein Maize (#186) Color C

Crochet hook size K10.5/6.50mm,

or size needed to obtain gauge

Tapestry needle

GAUGE:

5 rounds in pattern stitch = 4" (10cm)

ABBREVIATIONS:

beg = beginning

ch = chain

hdc = half double crochet

sc = single crochet

sl st = slip stitch

Special Stitch Instructions:

Reverse Single Crochet: swing hook across the fabric from left to right, the back of the hook will now be pointed up and left, the hook will be pointed down and right. Insert hook in the next stitch to the right, draw yarn through the stitch. , yarn over and through both loops on the hook. Insert in next stitch to the right and repeat above all the way around. Join with slip stitch and fasten off.

Changing colors: insert hook into last stitch using old color, switch to new color to finish last step of that stitch.

Repeats: from * to * for pattern repeats on each round.

With Color A, ch 3, join with sl st to form ring.	
Round 1:	make 8 sc in ring, ch 1.
Round 2:	2 hdc in each st around to end. Join with sl st to beg. stitch now and on each round after this. (16 hdcs)
Round 3:	Chain 1, hdc in first st, *2 hdc in next st, hdc in next st* around to end. (24 hdcs)
Round 4:	Ch 1, hdc in first 2 sts, *2 hdc in next st, hdc in next 2 sts* around to end. (32 hdcs)
Round 5:	Ch 1, hdc in first 3 sts, *2 hdc in next st, hdc in next 3 sts* around to end. (40 hdcs)
Round 6:	Ch 1, hdc in first 4 sts, *2 hdc in next st, hdc in next 4 sts* around to end. (48 hdcs)
Round 7:	Ch 1, hdc in first 5 sts, *2 hdc in next st, hdc in next 5 sts* around to end. (56 hdcs)
Rounds 8 and 9:	Hdc in each st around to end. Change to Color B at the end of Round 9, cut Color A. (56 hdcs)
Round 10:	Ch 1, (sc in next 13 sts, 2 sc in next st) 4 times. **TURN** (60 scs)
Round 11:	Ch 1, sc in first st, *draw up a loop in same st, draw up a loop in next st, yo, pull through all 3 loops on the hook* around to end, change to Color C. **DO NOT TURN**. Do not cut Color B. (60 scs)
Round 12:	Ch 1, hdc in first st, *yo, pull up a loop in same st, yo, pull up a loop in next st, yo, pull through all 5 loops on the hook* around to end, change to Color B. **TURN**. Do not cut color C. (60 hdcs)
Round 13:	Ch 1, sc around to end. **TURN**.
Round 14:	Repeat Round 11, then **TURN**. (60 scs)

The next three rounds are worked by alternating Color B and Color C for each stitch, starting the stitch with one color, finishing that stitch with the second color. The next stitch starts with the color of the loop on the hook, and finishes with the other color.

This could tighten your gauge quite a bit if you tug too hard. Try to keep a "light touch" when changing colors, or use the next size up crochet hook for this section, returning to smaller hook after Round 17.

You can do this one of two ways: alternate the starting stitch color each round for a zigzag type pattern, or start with the same color each round for a diagonal line pattern.

Rounds 15-17:	Sc around to end, join with slip stitch, ch 1. DO NOT TURN. (60 scs) At end of Round 17, change to Color B only.
Round 18	(Sc in next 10 sts, 2 sc in next st) 6 times. TURN. (66 scs)
Round 19:	Repeat Round 11. DO NOT TURN. (66 scs)
Round 20:	Repeat Round 12. TURN. Cut Color C at this point. (66 hdcs)
Round 21:	Repeat Round 13. TURN. (66 scs)
Round 22:	Repeat Round 11, change to Color A. TURN. Cut Color B at this point. (66 scs)
Rounds 23-25:	Ch 1, sc around to end. DO NOT TURN at end of rounds.
Round 26:	1, reverse sc around to end. Fasten off, weave in loose ends.

Note from the Big Cheese:

I really like this project, for new and old hands to have a fun, non-time intensive color changing project.

Even though it's rated easy for people who have worked in multiple colors, don't let that stop you if you haven't changed colors before. I think this would be a great project to try out color work!

Joanna Fingerless Mitts

by Shirley MacDonald (cherryred)

Materials:

Yarn: DK (sport weight) or aran (worsted weight) yarn of your choice

Hook: 4mm for DK/Sport or 4.5mm for aran/worsted

Gloves are worked side to side in a mix of single (sc) & half double (hdc) crochet rib which means gauge isn't too important as they can be sized to fit anyone either by adding or decreasing stitches or rows. The combination of the two stitches produces a snug cuff.

 If you prefer a looser cuff you can work in half double crochet rib throughout. To lengthen or shorten the gloves simply increase or decrease the base chain, making sure that you have an odd number of working stitches so that they lace up evenly. The mock lace-up effect is worked last & takes the place of seaming. They work well in different weights of yarn

. Photo shows glove worked in Twilleys Freedom Spirit.

Base chain	36 chain
Row 1	1 half double crochet in 2nd chain from hook, 1 hdc in each ch to end, turn - 35 sts
Row 2	Working in back loops only of previous row: ch 1 (does not count as 1st stitch), 1 single crochet (sc) in each of first 15 stitches, 1 hdc in each of rem 20 stitches to end, turn - 35 sts
Row 3	Working in back loops only of previous row: ch1 (does not count as 1st stitch), 1 hdc in each stitch to end, turn - 35 sts
Row 4 onwards	Repeat rows 2 & 3 until work covers back of hand from outer edge to base of thumb, ending with a row 3
Thumb hole row 1	Working in back loops only of previous row: 1 ch (does not count as 1st stitch), 1 sc in first 15 sts, 1 hdc in each of next 4 sts, 6 ch, miss next 6 sts, 1 hdc in each of next 10 sts to end of row, turn
Thumb hole row 2	Working in back loops only of previous row: 1 ch (does not count as 1st stitch), 1 hdc in each of next 10 sts, 1 hdc in each of next 6 ch, 1 hdc in each of rem 19 sts to end, turn - 35 sts

Side Two Row A	Working in back loops only of previous row: ch 1 (does not count as 1st stitch), 1 single crochet (sc) in each of first 15 stitches, 1 hdc in each of rem 20 stitches to end, turn - 35 sts
Row B	Working in back loops only of previous row: ch1 (does not count as 1st stitch), 1 hdc in each stitch to end, turn - 35 sts
Row C onwards	Repeat rows A & B until you have worked the same amount of rows as on side 1

Lace up row	Fold glove in half, matching foundation row to last row worked. Chain 2, slip stitch in 1st stitch of foundation row. Turn work & slip stitch in next 2 stitches of foundation row. *Chain 2, miss next stitch of last row worked, slip stitch in next stitch of last row worked, slip stitch in next 2 stitches of last row worked, turn work. Chain 2, miss next stitch of foundation row, slip stitch in next stitch of foundation row. Turn work & slip stitch in next 2 stitches of foundation row. Continue from * until glove is fully 'laced-up' finishing off by joining the last stitch of foundation row & last row worked with a chain 2, slip stitch.
Finishing off	Fasten off yarn & weave in ends.

Stash Mountain

Art by Kristin Kesecker (technogoddess)

Bah...Ram...and You!
By Alia Smith (Crotcheteer)

I'd done this sort of thing before...travelling someplace I had never been to learn about something I knew little to nothing about. It's a pattern with me. Some might say... a sickness not unlike my overuse of ellipses.

This time, I was to board a bus from somewhere inside Philadelphia which was bound for a destination somewhere outside Baltimore for the purpose of attending a Sheep and Wool Festival

What's a sheep and wool festival? I'm glad you asked. It's sort of like a mass introduction of one group of people - The producers of yarn and yarn-related anythings with their equal and opposite counterparts - the people who wish to buy them.

As with anything, there are some who would consider the prospect of a Sheep and Wool Festival to be oxymoronic at best (the OAB's) and others who get very, very excited about it (the VVE's) I was about to board a bus with 100 VVE's followed closely by another 100 in separate bus, all setting sail from one little yarn shop.

Even odder, no doubt, to the OAB's is the fact that we must have leapfrogged 10 other buses full of VVE's on the way down. Since I'm not a spinner or a knitter, most of the conversation was foreign to me so I kept quiet except for an occasional expletive when I dropped my hook and a "thank you" when it was returned to me.

Note from the Big Cheese:

CLF SNORT ALERT! Don't drink coffee, tea or anything else when reading this story!

(*For those not on the CLF Message board on Ravelry.com,* **we put snort alerts on our messages to give fair warning, and save keyboards!**)

I did manage to ask someone if that was a Mike-n-Ike under their seat or did they lose a needle covery thing. It was a Mike-n-Ike.

Anyway, the event.

I go to these sorts of things to learn stuff, but also to reconnect myself with humanity at large and to remind myself that I am neither the most fashion challenged person on the planet, nor the oddest looking one.

Everyone except me, it would seem, had something that they had created on or about their persons. There were sweaters, tops, shawls, belts, headbands, headwraps, skirts, bags, swaddling clothes, you name it.

To me, it was like walking the streets of a bazaar in a country I had never been to. Constant chatter hummed around me broken only by the occasional MMMMMMBLEEEEEAAAAAGGGHHH of a sheep or ram. (Ram, by the way, have freakishly large testicles. I'm pretty sure that a hollowed out sheep nut could house an Indonesian family.)

There were shouts of glee at the prices a particular yarn hawker was offering. There were shouts of recognition as old friends and cyber-friends recognized each other across paddocks. There were shouts of "Oh, crap!" as those distracted by all the colorful string walked right into fresh piles of sheep poop.

What struck me most is that fiber artists are such a diverse group that we cannot be stereotyped. The common images of the crunchy patchouli-soaked weaver or the librarian knitter or the crocheter with as many cats as grandchildren just don't hold up.

We come in as many colors and weights and fibers as there were yarns available at this gig and we do just about as many things with it all. As for me, I took some time to see all this through my camera lens and then set about doing some shopping.

Most notable of my purchases is a skein of "naked" wool yarn for the purpose of dyeing it myself with Kool-Aid. Apparently it's not just for deranged cult leaders anymore!

I also came home with a sunburn that looked not unlike a yoke around my neck, but that's alright. I have bigger worries...most importantly, how I can get a note to the U.N. about having solved the world housing crisis through sheep testicle technology.

The Simple Yet Versatile Scarf Recipe

by Barbara Hillery Van Elsen aka Altobarb

The Basic Pattern

I love creating freeform items. I love the special kind of concentration it takes. But sometimes I'm just not up to coordinating all the factors that go into making good freeform. And sometimes I have to make something for someone who doesn't quite "get" all that freeform can be. Or I'm teaching someone who finds freeform intimidating. So I came up with this scarf recipe.

Using this recipe and a solid color yarn, you can make a classic-looking scarf, but if you change color each row and concentrate on finding good matches for the colors and fibers in your work, it will be a knockout! You don't have to be concerned with shapes or stitches or fit, as in regular freeform, but just with finding the perfect next yarn to use. And the fun part is that, while the front and back both look lovely, they look different! (This is because every other row only peeks out between the adjoining colors.)

This scarf is very versatile and, in a solid color, produces a scarf with classic ribbing that is suitable for men or women. I used Woolpak 10 ply (slightly thicker than worsted) with a J hook and made a good-sized men's scarf in about 3 hours. Another version used a G hook with sport-weight baby alpaca and took longer but made a finer and very luxurious scarf.

Make a nice, loose chain as LONG as you want the scarf to be (you'll be working up and down the scarf, not across) and then add 2 chains. (If you're not sure how long you want your scarf, one guideline suggests making it as long as the wearer.)

Row 1. Skip 2 chains and make a half double crochet into the 3rd chain from your hook.

Working into the back bump, make one hdc in each chain to the end of the row.

Chain 2 and turn.

Row 2. Hdc into both loops of the first stitch. Working into the back loop only, hdc in each stitch of the row, except for the last stitch, which is worked through both loops.

The Semi-Freeform Scarf

Start by choosing a favorite color or two. No more than two for now. Find at least three yarns that are predominately the colors you choose. You won't need a lot of each yarn, so remainders from other projects are perfect. Vary the fibers—make sure you have at least one regular plain yarn, one fuzzy (I like to use lots of angora for a very pettable scarf) and one shiny yarn in each color. And, very important, don't forget this is a scarf and will rest on the owner's neck—it cannot scratch. In truth, you can have one or two scratchy rows, but they'll have to be worked carefully between fuzzy soft rows—best to start out with only soft feeling yarns.

Now choose your unifying color. If you're only starting with one color, that's easy. The unifying color will keep your scarf from looking like you didn't think about it at all. A little planning here can make a huge difference in your finished product.

Next, you want to choose your edge yarn. It should be in the unifying color and will be the first and last rows of the scarf, so be sure you have enough of that yarn (though if you have exactly the same color in a different yarn and different fiber, that's OK, too). It should be especially soft, since the wearer will feel the yarn on the edges more than the inside rows.

Using your edge yarn, make a chain an inch or so longer than you want the scarf to be. (Don't forget that you can do fringe or an edging on the long ends to make it longer if needed.) Follow the directions for Row 1

Now you have another choice to make. Decide if you want fringe and if so, how long. That is how long you want to make each yarn end when you end and start new yarns on each row. Yes, you will use a different yarn each row. You might repeat some, but not next to each other.

Join a different yarn and follow the directions for Row 2. End off yarn.

Join a different yarn and follow the directions for Row 2. End off yarn. Continue until the scarf is as wide as you want it As you choose your next yarn, look to vary fiber and color; make sure the yarn looks right on both sides. I always do a test inch or two in the yarn I think I want next and then carefully examine both sides of the scarf to see if it really harmonizes in both texture and color. You may be surprised to find the colors going in places you didn't know they would. You might start with all peaceful colors and halfway through find it screaming for a spot of color from the opposite side of the color wheel. Or you may find you just want to use a touch of color and a lot of neutrals. Or use black every other row or so to punch up the other colors.

And fiber—if you use a fuzzy yarn, another yarn and a fuzzy yarn, the two fuzzies will block almost all of the other color from the fuzzy side. This presents lots of possibilities—what if you made a scarf where every other row was fuzzy and the intervening rows smooth. Each type of yarn would end up on one side of the scarf—and the fuzzy yarn will poke through to the smooth side, while the smooth yarn would barely be visible from the fuzzy side.

Don't forget that some sparkle adds dimension. As does some boucle or chenille.

Make one last row in your edge yarn. Or edge color in a different yarn. End off. Admire your creation.

Edging options

I usually don't put any edging on the long sides of my scarf, but you could if you wanted to. I find that the colors and fibers are decorative enough. I do like to vary the treatment of the short ends, though. Here are some suggestions:

 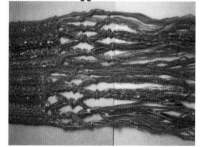 

Origami Socks

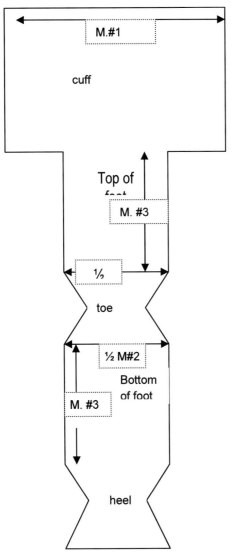

cuff

M.#1

Top of foot

M. #3

½

toe

½ M#2

Bottom of foot

M. #3

heel

By Deborah E. Burger (aka Cerdeb)

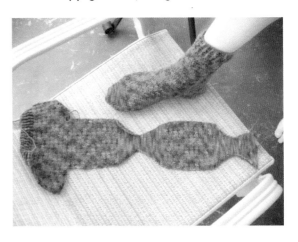

Comfy, close fitting socks to crochet, which will fit into shoes! The shaping is done flat, in rows, so "turning the heel" is much simpler than in many sock patterns.

Difficulty: Intermediate (contains increases, decreases and 2 pattern stitches besides single crochet).

Materials: sock weight yarn; I used Schachenmayr nomotta Regia Design Line Kaffe Fassett, approx. 1 skein.
     F crochet hook, or hook to meet gauge.
     Darning or yarn needle
Gauge: 19 sts. And 17 rows in crunch pattern stitch = 4 in.

Pattern Stitches:

1. FPDC ribbing-- (turning chain counts as first stitch in each row) Ch. Desired length, plus 2 ch. <u>Row 1</u>- work 1 dc in 4th ch from hook, and each ch across. Ch 3, turn. <u>Row 2-</u> *fpdc in first dc, bpdc in next dc. Repeat from *
across row. Ch 3, turn. <u>Row 3 and following</u>- Repeat Row 2, making fpdc in fpdc and bpdc in bpdc.
   Crunch stitch—*sc in first stitch, dc in next. Repeat from * across row, ending with a dc. Ch 1, turn.
   Repeat Row 1 to desired length.

Notes: The sock is crocheted in one flat piece, and the finished piece will resemble the diagram. I have included my measurements, which are for a size 9 ½ foot, which takes a regular commercial "9-11" women's sock.

Size changes are made by adjusting to the dimensions of the intended foot, so before beginning to crochet, make the following measurements, and write them down:

- **M1:** around ankle or calf at what will be the top of the sock cuff. (model is 8", for a crew length sock)_____
- **M2:** around foot at "ball joint", 2" from end of longest toe. (model is 9 ½ ") _____
- **M3:** "crease to crease" down top of instep from ankle crease to ball, or base of toes. (model is 5") _____

M4: diagonally around heel and ankle from back of heel around top of foot at ankle crease. (model is 12 ½")

Adjustments for unique foot shapes: If your intended foot is very wide, narrow, or has particularly long or short toes, or a very high instep, please read through the adjustments at the end of the pattern, and decide which ones you will need to make. Best to do this before you start, because the sock is not easy to flatten out again, once it's sewn together.

Directions:

Starting at top of cuff, make a fairly loose chain as long as M1 (don't stretch the chain in measuring), and add 2 ch Make sure you have ended with an even number of chains. If not, add 1 extra to make an even number.(model was 46 ch to make 8", therefore chain 48).

Rows 1-4: work FPDC ribbing for 4 rows. At end of Row 4, ch1, turn.

Rows 5 to bottom of "leg": work in Crunch Stitch, starting every row with a sc and ending every row with dc, ch1, turn. When piece

is as "tall" as you want the leg part of the sock, fasten off at the end of a row, leaving a 12" tail for sewing later. (Model cuff was 16

rows tall)

Top of Foot: Now comes a bit of "tricky arithmetic", pencil or calculator at the ready! You need to mark your last row, so that ½ of M2 is centered in the row. For example, the model's M2 is 9 ½ ", so I found the center of the crocheted cuff, and measured ¼ of that distance to either side of the center, which means finding the stitch nearest to 2 3/8" from each side of center.) With right side facing, join yarn at the first marked stitch with a sc and work an even number of stitches in crunch stitch, across to your second marker. If your marker is at a double crochet, work one more stitch so that your current row ends with a dc. Ch1, turn. (the model's row for top of foot was 24 stitches,   4 ¾", half of M2. So the markers were placed to skip the first 11 sts in the row, and to leave the last11 sts unworked). Continue to work in Crunch Stitch until your "top of foot section" is as long as M3. Write your number of rows here_____. (Model's was 20 rows, to closely match the 5" length). At end, ch1, turn.

Toe: The toe decrease/increase is worked in plain old sc.

Decrease-- Work the first toe row even, (same number of stitches you have been working—model's was 24). Row 2 (and all even rows)- sc 2 together (1 decrease) at beginning AND END of row, ch 1, turn. Row 3 (and all odd rows)—work even. Continue decrease and even rows till you have worked 2" of sc. On the model sock, that reduced the stitch count to 10 sts in the final row.

Increase Row 1-- Work one more row, even. Ch 1, turn.

Now, reverse shaping: Row 2, and all even rows, will be increase rows: work 2 sc in first stitch AND in last stitch of row, ch 1, turn. Row 3 and all odd rows, work even. Continue till toe increase matches toe decrease. You will be back to your original number of stitches from the foot section (the model was 24) and will have two sections with diagonal sides that are opposite each other (see diagram). Work final row of sc over that number of sts, ch1, turn.

Bottom of foot: work exactly as top of foot—Crunch St. on your "even number" of stitches, ending every row with dc, ch1, turn. Work till bottom of foot exactly matches top of foot.

Heel: The heel decrease/increase section is worked EXACTLY the same as the toe section. At end, fasten off leaving a 12" tail for sewing. Ta-dah!!! You should have a crocheted piece that looks like the one in the diagram.

Sewing: With Wrong side facing out (you decide at this point which will be the right and wrong side. It hasn't mattered till now, but now you must choose and stick with your choice.) whip stitch a seam from top to bottom of the leg/cuff portion of the sock. If you make small stitches, matching the stitches of each row, with the same yarn, this seam will be nearly invisible. Fasten off. Next, fold the heel section so that the diagonal edges of each side are together, and with wrong side facing out, sew them. Next, fold the toe section the same way, and starting at the toe, sew each side seam so that the top of the foot exactly matches the bottom of the foot. You will end the seam when you meet the diagonal seam of the heel. It should look more or less like a sock at this point. Finally, center the end of the heel section across the back half of the leg/cuff, and sew together. Weave in all ends (be careful not to leave

any knots, because when you are walking on them, they will be uncomfortable!). Turn your sock right side out, and slip on to your foot!

Additional adjustments for uniquely shaped feet: If you have particularly heavy or skinny ankles/calves, or very wide feet, very long or short toes, or a very high instep, the proportions may be a bit off. To find out if this will be a problem, and to make the sock fit the foot, here are some adjustments you can make:

1.   M1 + ½ of M2 need to be roughly equal to M4 for the sock to fit. If this is not true of your foot, and you have more than ½ inch of difference, you may have to compromise with a little looseness at the bottom of the leg/cuff. However, the stitch pattern has enough body, in a wool blend, sock-weight yarn, to keep from falling down, even if it's not quite as snug as a knitted sock. The important thing is for the rib to fit the calf, and for the sock to stretch over M4 (largest width of foot).
2.   After crocheting the original 4 rows of ribbing, stretch it, and see if you can get your "M1" rib to stretch to nearly the length of M4. If it's more than half an inch too short, add a few stitches to the WIDTH of each section f the sock, still maintaining an even number of stitches in each row. If it doesn't need any stretching at all (that is, it's more than ½ in. too long), you may want to subtract a few stitches the width of each section, still keeping rows on an even number of stitches.
3.   You can play with changing hook size, too. If the foot part needs to be narrower in relation to the leg/cuff, just switch to a hook one or two sizes smaller for working the foot. If the foot needs to be wider in relation to the leg/cuff, use a slightly larger hook for that section.
4.   If your toes are particularly long, or particularly short, a good fit can be obtained by adjusting the length of the toe decrease/increase section. You can inc/dec more often for shorter toes (less than 2" from base to end of toe), or inc/dec less often for longer toes (more than 2" from base to end of toe). DO NOT repeat this adjustment on the heel section, because heels are really pretty standard in shape!

For a foot with very wide toe section, you may want to dec/inc less often, and make your final row wider than the 10 stitches suggested, perhaps 12 or even 14 stitches. A sock needs to be snug to fit in the shoe without wrinkling, but it should not constrict or pinch the toes, or have to stretch so tightly that the individual stitches feel like little knots when walking on them! Again, if you make this adjustment, do not repeat it on the heel section

Eleanora's Arm Warmers

By Darlisa Riggs aka Fignations

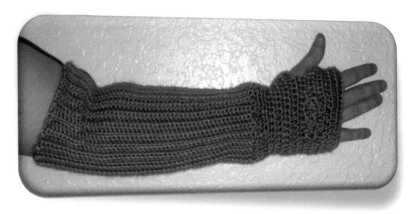

Example made with Red Heart Ltd. Soft Yarn Solids in Guacamole

Sizes & Materials List:

Hook(s): Use recommended hook size for yarn being used
Yarn: Any weight yarn such as sport, worsted, etc., 1-2 skeins

Examples made using Red Heart Ltd. Soft Yarn Solids in Guacamole, Patons SWS in Natural Navy, and Mountain Colors Mountain Goat in Sweetpea.

Tapestry Needle

Gauge: None

Since moving from Houston to Salt Lake City, I've become obsessed with arm and wrist warmers. When I first started looking for patterns, they were extremely hard to locate but since I've joined Ravelry, patterns for them seem to be coming out of the woodwork, both for knit and crochet versions. Of course, that doesn't mean I can't be greedy and want even more!

This pattern was created for a friend of mine who wanted arm wamers that covered her knuckles and went above her elbows. The pattern provides a recipe for crocheting your own arm or wrist warmers, depending on how long you want them to be and how much of your hand you want covered. Gauge is not important and you can pretty much use whatever yarn and hook you want. Crochet loose or tight, lacy or not, adult, teen, or child sizes ... your choice.

Example below made with Patons SWS yarn in Natural Navy

Cuff (Right or Left Mitt)	
Base Chain	Measure from the base of your palm to where you'd like the arm warmer to end below then elbow, then measure around your arm at that point for the circumference. Leave a tail long enough to sew up the sleeve of the mitt and crochet a ch long enough to match the length measurement, plus 1 ch.
Row 1	Sc in second ch from hook and in each ch across, ch 1, turn.
Row 2	Sc in back loop of first sc and in each sc across, ch 1, turn.
Row 3 to end	Repeat row 2 until end length matches the circumference measurement you made. For a loose fit, don't stretch the ribbing as you measure. For a tighter fit, slightly stretch the fabric to reach the circumference measurement.
	The point where you stop will be the wrist edge. Join with a sl st to the last st made to the stitch on the opposite side of the wrist edge to form a circle. The rest of the mitt will be done in the round, joining each row with a sl st.
Wrist (Right or Left Mitt)	
Row 1	Ch 1, sc in end of each row around, join with sl st in first sc.
Row 2	Ch 1, sc in first sc, sc in next sc, *sc2tog, sc in next 2 sc,* repeat from * to * around, joining with sl st to first sc. Depending on the number of ribbing rows you did, you may end with the sc2tog or just one sc instead of two sc as the last sts.
	Test mitt to see if the wrist fits comfortably. If it is too large, do another row or two of decreases.
Last wrist row	Ch 1, sc in first sc and in each sc around. Join with sl st in first sc.
Thumb Increases	
Row 1	Ch 2 (beg hdc), hdc in next sc and in each sc around. Hdc in same sc as beg hdc. Join with sl st in second ch of beg hdc.
Row 2	Repeat row 1. (If you have a small hand, you can skip row 2 if needed.) For left mitt, skip down to "Left Mitt" section.
Right Mitt	
	Fold mitt in half with seam at center on underside of mitt. Mark left side of mitt. Section over the seam will be for the palm area, section over the left marker will be for thumb.
Row 3	Ch 2, hdc in each hdc around until you reach the st marked for the thumb, 2 hdc in marked hdc and in next hdc, hdc in next hdc and in each hdc to end. Join with sl st in second ch of beg hdc.
Row 4	Ch 2, hdc in each hdc around until you reach the first hdc of the first inc on row 3, 2 hdc in this hdc, hdc in next hdc, 2 hdc in next hdc, hdc in next hdc and in each hdc to end. Join with sl st in second ch of beg hdc.

Row 5	Ch 2, hdc in each hdc around until you reach the first hdc of the first inc on row 4, 2 hdc in this hdc, hdc in next hdc, 2 hdc in next hdc, hdc in next hdc and in each hdc to end. Join with sl st in second ch of beg hdc.
	Check length of mitt to where increases cover base of thumb. If more coverage is needed, repeat row 5.
Row 6	Ch 2, hdc in each hdc around until you reach the third st to the right of the thumb marker, ch 10 *(9 if less room is needed)*, skip next 7 sts (3 to right of thumb center, thumb center, and 3 to left of thumb center), hdc in next hdc and in each hdc to end. Join with sl st in second ch of beg hdc.
	Put on mitt with thumb through thumb opening and seam on underside of palm. Adjust mitt on hand until it feels comfortable in thum area. Mark approximate center of mitt on back of the hand. Count 4 sts to right of front center marker and mark this st.
Row 7	Ch 2, hdc in each hdc around until you reach the marked hdc to the right of the center marker, skip marked hdc, fan st (2 dc, ch 1, 2dc) in next hdc, skip 2 hdc, fan st in next hdc, skip 2 hdc, fan st in next hdc, skip next hdc, hdc in each remaining hdc before thumb opening then in each ch across opening and each hdc after opening to end. Join with sl st in second ch of beg hdc.
	Tip: If mitt is too loose at base of thumb over palm, decrease using hdc2tog at edge of thumb opening next to palm. This can be done on rows 7, 8, and/or 9.
Row 8	Ch 2, hdc in each hdc to first shell st, hdc in first dc, fan st in ch sp of each fan st on previous row, hdc in last dc of third fan st and in each hdc to approx center st of thumb opening, hdc2tog in center st of thumb opening, hdc in next hdc and in each hdc to end. Join with sl st in second ch of beg hdc.
Row 9	Ch 2, hdc in each hdc to first dc of first fan st on previous row, hdc in first dc, hdc in ch sp of first fan st, hdc in sp between first and second fan st, hdc in ch sp of second fan st, hdc in sp between second and third fan st, hdc in ch space of third fan st, hdc in last dc of third fan st, hdc in next hdc and in each hdc to end. Join with sl st in second ch of beg hdc.
Row 10	Ch 2, hdc in each hdc around. Join with sl st in second ch of beg hdc.
Row 11	Check length of mitt to see if it covers enough of your hand and/or knuckles. To add more length, repeat row 10 until it is long enough for you.
Left Mitt	
	Fold mitt in half with seam at center on underside of mitt. Mark right side of mitt. Section over the seam will be for the palm area, section over the right marker will be for thumb.
Row 3	Ch 2, hdc in each hdc around until you reach the st before the one marked for the thumb, 2 hdc in this hdc and in next (marked) hdc, hdc in next hdc and in each hdc to end. Join with sl st in second ch of beg hdc.
Row 4	Ch 2, hdc in each hdc around until you reach the second hdc of the first inc on row 3, 2 hdc in this hdc, hdc in next hdc, 2 hdc in next hdc, hdc in next hdc and in each hdc to end. Join with sl st in second ch of beg hdc.

Row 5	Ch 2, hdc in each hdc around until you reach the second hdc of the first inc on row 4, 2 hdc in this hdc, hdc in next hdc, 2 hdc in next
	hdc, hdc in next hdc and in each hdc to end. Join with sl st in second ch of beg hdc.
	Check length of mitt to where increases cover base of thumb. If more coverage is needed, repeat row 5.
Row 6	Ch 2, hdc in each hdc around until you reach the third st to the right of the thumb marker, ch 10 (9 if less room is needed), skip next 7 sts (3 to right of thumb center, thumb center, and 3 to left of thumb center), hdc in next hdc and in each hdc to end. Join with sl st in second ch of beg hdc.
	Put on mitt with thumb through thumb opening and seam on underside of palm. Adjust mitt on hand until it feels comfortable in thum area. Mark approximate center of mitt on back of the hand. Count 4 sts to right of front center marker and mark this st.
Row 7	Ch 2, hdc in each hdc around and in each ch across thumb opening until you reach the marked hdc to the right of the center marker, skip marked hdc, fan st (2 dc, ch 1, 2dc) in next hdc, skip 2 hdc, fan st in next hdc, skip 2 hdc, fan st in next hdc, skip next hdc, hdc in each remaining hdc to end. Join with sl st in second ch of beg hdc.
	Tip: If mitt is too loose at base of thumb over palm, decrease using hdc2tog at edge of thumb opening next to palm. This can be done on rows 7, 8, and/or 9.
Row 8	Ch 2, hdc in each hdc *to approx center st of thumb opening, hdc2tog in center st of thumb opening, hdc in next hdc and in each hdc to first* shell st, hdc in first dc, fan st in ch sp of each fan st on previous row, hdc in last dc of third fan st and in each hdc to end. Join with sl st in second ch of beg hdc.
Row 9	Ch 2, hdc in each hdc to first dc of first fan st on previous row, hdc in first dc, hdc in ch sp of first fan st, hdc in sp between first and second fan st, hdc in ch sp of second fan st, hdc in sp between second and third fan st, hdc in ch space of third fan st, hdc in last dc of third fan st, hdc in next hdc and in each hdc to end. Join with sl st in second ch of beg hdc.
Row 10	Ch 2, hdc in each hdc around. Join with sl st in second ch of beg hdc.
	Check length of mitt to see if it covers enough of your hand and/or knuckles. To add more length, repeat row 10 until it is long enough for you.

Finishing:
Bind off. Turn mitt inside out and sew up seam using the beg tail you left when starting the mitt. Weave in ends.

Keep Your Hands Healthy When Hooking

By Andee Graves (aka Mamas2Hands)

Does crocheting have to hurt? Will there come a time when you will have to relegate your hooks to the dustbin of past joys because age and infirmity have taken their toll? Maybe not. There are a number of simple strategies that we can incorporate into our crochet work to improve our chances of avoiding injury from our crafting.

Finding and implementing hand healthy changes that are right for your life and crafting style can be an enlightening adventure. Changing how you work and your tools can be a bit tricky, but once you've got the hang of any new approaches your hands will thank you. The biggest issue for many crafters is the limited crafting time we have in our day, so losing current productivity to a learning curve can be frustrating. If you can keep your eye on the bigger goal, longevity with your beloved craft, the frustration is more bearable.

1. Find a hand friendly hook

The term ergonomic gets thrown around a lot these days. Sometimes it can be hard to know if the claim is even accurate for every item labeled as such. Ergonomic comes from two Greek words; ergon, meaning work, and nomoi, meaning natural laws. Combined they create a word that defines the science of work and a person's relationship to that work. The general idea is to create a comfortable and efficient interface between human and machine.

Now, not too many of us are accustomed to thinking of our crochet hooks as a machine, but they really are. Our hooks are a simple machine, they allow us to create fabric from any type of flexible pliable thread-like substance with seeming magic. Have you ever tried making a long chain with just your fingers? Then you know how your hook can speed the process, as well as making it quick to build upon that base chain to create elaborate stitches.

There are loads of hooks available on the market, and trying a variety seems to be the best method for finding your dream hook. If you live near a yarn store that has a good variety of hooks stocked, check if you can "test drive" some in the shop. This way you know if you're going to like them before making the investment. Better yet check with your crochet friends to see what hooks they have and if you can borrow a few of them. Remember, even if your friend has a hook style they despise, it could be *your* dream hook. Differences in hand size, working tension, yarn choice and body mechanics can really impact which hook is going to be more comfortable for different people.

You can also make your own ergonomic hook by changing a current hook. There are many different approaches. This can be as simple as putting a band-aid on the area of your hook that makes your hand sore or making a customized wide handle using polymer clay. HilaryGermany on the Ravelry site has an awesome informative tutorial on her blog about this method.

You can also make your own ergonomic hook by changing a current hook. There are many different approaches. This can be as simple as putting a band-aid on the area of your hook that makes your hand sore or making a customized wide handle using polymer clay. HilaryGermany on the Ravelry site has an awesome informative tutorial on her blog about this method.

Commercial Ergonomic/Hand Friendly Hooks

Addi Turbos – Sold in a number of online stores and many local yarn stores.

Brittany Hooks – Sold in a number of online stores and many local yarn stores.
www.brittanyneedles.com

Clover Soft Touch & Clover Lites hooks - Can usually purchase them at Michaels, JoAnns
and Hobby Lobby or similar shops, as well as numerous
online stores.

Clover Reflections Hook Sets – New product from Clover can order from www.clover-
usa.com

Eleggant Crochet hook – Interchangable handle with 6 hooks available online
http://bourbj.tripod.com/

Susan Bates aluminum hooks with Bamboo handles – Available at most all Susan Bates
outlets online and in stores.

Laurel Hill Crochet Hooks – Sometimes difficult to locate, these are sold in some online
stores and local yarn stores.

Kollage Square hooks – www.kollageyarns.com

Jimbo hooks – Jimbo is a Ravelry member you can order his hooks through his Blog at
http://jimbosfrontporch.blogspot.com/

Provo Craft Interchangable Ergonomic Handle

Turn of the Century hooks – www.turn-of-the-century.com

There are many more, search the discussion boards for Hook Reviews and follow the links to
discover your "dream" hook.

Saucy!

By Melissa Mall aka Melissa

I love this hat. It's so fast, so simple, and just so saucy. It can be worn a few different ways: to the back like a slouch, to the side like a beret, or to the front like a newsboy. When made in different yarns, the personality of the hat completely changes - and at about 90 minutes a pop, you'll want to make one in all your favorite fibers! I've already made it five times, and here's a tip: when choosing a yarn for your Saucy hat, make sure you pick something with some drape. A stiff yarn won't allow the hat to slouch.

Green hat made with approx. 100yds Lion Brand Lion Chenille in Sage: [174yds/157m per 3oz/85g skein]

Red Hat made with approx. 100yds Mondial Merino Plus in Scarlet: [137yds/125m per 3/5oz/100g skein]

J/10 (6mm) hook

Yarn needle

Gauge: 12sts x 8 rows in hdc = 4"

Abbreviations:

ch – chain

dec – decrease (pull up a loop in each of next 2 sts and work as one)

hdc – half-double crochet

inc – increase (make 2 sts in next st)

sc – single crochet

sl st – slip stitch

US pattern conventions used

Note: <u>Do not</u> join rounds unless directed.

Rnd 1: Ch 3; make 10 hdc in 3rd ch from hook. (10 hdc)
Rnd 2: [Hdc inc] 10 times. (20 hdc)
Rnd 3: [Hdc, hdc inc] 10 times. (30 hdc)
Rnd 4: [Hdc 2, hdc inc] 10 times. (40 hdc)
Rnd 5: [Hdc 3, hdc inc] 10 times. (50 hdc)
Rnd 6: [Hdc 4, hdc inc] 10 times. (60 hdc)
Rnd 7: [Hdc 5, hdc inc] 10 times. (70 hdc)
Rnds 8-11: Hdc around. (70 hdc)
Rnd 12: [Hdc 5, hdc dec] 10 times. (60 hdc)
Rnd 13: [Hdc 4, hdc dec] 10 times. (50 hdc)
Rnd 14: [Hdc 3, hdc dec] 10 times. (40 hdc)
Rnd 15: Sl st, ch 1. Sc in same st. Sc 7, sc dec. [Sc 8, sc dec] 3 more times. (36 sc) Join round.
Rnd 16: Ch 1, sc around. (36 sc) Join round.

Brim:

Row 1: Ch 1, sc, hdc inc. [hdc, hdc inc] 2 times, sc. (10 sts) Sl st across next 2 sts, turn.
Row 2: Ch 1, sc 2. Hdc inc, hdc 8, hdc inc. Sc 2. (16 sts) Sl st across next 2 sts, turn.
Row 3: Skip 1st sl st; sl st in next st. Sc, sc inc, sc 12. Sc inc, sc, sl st in next st. (20 sts) Finish off, weave in ends.

fun~n~Games

Feed Me an open-ended game for toddlers and a way to use your swatches.

By Karla McCalmont (karlaamm)

When teaching myself to crochet, I worked through many of the stitch samples and motifs in the *Readers' Digest Complete Guide to Needlework* chapter on crochet. I made them out of a variety of colors of yarn or thread. I didn't know what to do with them after I made them. I didn't want to throw them away, I thought the kids could use them somehow. They sort of played with them, but it wasn't until my husband put them into a small zippered pouch that the fun really began. We dumped them out, I puckered up the bag like lips and said "Feed me." My son tried to stuff the motifs in before I ate them and his fingers up. "Feed me, more! More! More!" With much excitement and giggles we played this game over and over and over. Sometimes I'll ask for all of the blue ones, then the green, the red, etc. until all of the colors have been eaten. Other times I ask for shapes. The kids learn their colors, shapes and improve their hand-eye coordination skills. Sometimes they practice the zipper, and sometimes they hold the bag and say, "Feed me."

Materials for playing the game:

Plastic Bag

Swatches and motifs

Family

Sense of humor

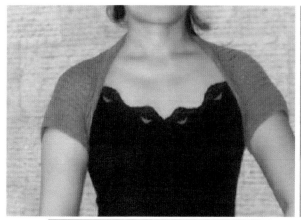

Skill level: Advanced beginner

Finished Measurement:

fits bust size Small- 32", Medium, 34", Large, 36"

Materials:
Crochet Cotton thread size 8, 2-3 balls

Crochet hook, size 2.5 mm, or 4/0 or size to obtain gauge

Abbreviations: **ch** = chain, **ss** = slip stitch, **sc** = single crochet, **dc** = double crochet,   **st** = stitch **rnd** = round

dc-tog = dc two stitches together – (Yo, insert hook into stitch, yo and pull up look, yo and pull thru 2 loops) twice, yo and pull thru remaining loops on hook.

A Little Cotton Shrug

By Mimi Alelis (aka Mimicat)

Shrug

Start with ch 79 (82, 85), ss to 1st ch to form a circle, being careful not to twist the chain.

Row 1: Ch 1, sc in each ch around. Join with ss on the 1st sc. (79, 82, 85 sc) Turn.

Row 2: (right side) Ch 3 (does not count as a st), dc on each sc around, with dc increase every 9 (10, 10) sts. Ss on top of beg ch 3. (87, 90, 93 dc) Turn.

Row 3: Ch 1, sc in each dc around. Ss on the 1st sc to join. (87, 90, 93 sc) Turn.

Row 4: Ch 3, dc in each sc around. Ss on top of beg ch 3. (87, 90, 93 dc) Turn.

Rows 5 & 6: Repeat rows 3 and 4.

Row 7: Repeat row 3.

Row 8: Ch 1, sc in 10 sc, hdc in next, dc in next 65 (68, 71) sc, hdc in next, sc in 10 sc. Ss on the 1st sc to join. (87, 90, 93 sts) Turn.

Row 9: Repeat row 3.

Row 10: Ch 1, sc in 20 sc, hdc in next, dc in next 45 (48, 51) sc, hdc in next, sc in 20 sc. Ss on the 1st sc to join. (87, 90, 93 sts) Turn.

Row 11: Repeat row 3.

Row 12: Ch 3, dc in each sc around. Do not join. (87, 90, 93 dc) Turn.

Row 13: Ch 2, skip the first 2 dc, sc on next dc, (ch 2, skip 2 dc, sc on next dc) repeat across. (29, 30, 31 ch-2 spaces) Turn.

Row 14: Ch 3 (now counts as 1st dc), 2 dc in 1st ch 2 space. 3 dc in each ch 2 space across. (87, 90, 93 dc) Turn.

Rows 15- 94 (size small), 15- 98 (medium), and 15- 102 (large): Repeat rows 13 & 14. At the end of last row, ss on top of beg ch 3 to join. Turn.

Next row: Repeat row 3. (87, 90, 93 sc)

Next 3 rows: Repeat rows 10, 9 and 8.

Next 4 rows: Repeat row 3 and 4, twice.

Next row: Repeat row 3.

Next row: Ch 3, dc on each sc around, with dc tog every 9th and 10th stitch (10th and 11th for med and large). Ss on top of beg ch 3. (79, 82, 85 dc) Turn.

Last row: Ch 1, sc in each st around. (79, 82, 85 sc) Fasten off.

Edging:

Rnd 1: With right side facing, join thread on at the middle of one underarm. Ch 1, working in ends of rows, (sc, ch 1) on each stitch around, with an additional sc on each underarm. Join with ss to 1st sc of this rnd. Turn.

Rnd 2: Ch 1, (sc in next 2 sts, sc tog the next 2 sts) repeat around, join. Turn.

Rnd 3: Ch 3, dc in each st around, with dc increase on each underarm, join. Turn.

Rnd 4: Ch 1, sc in each st around, join. Turn.

Rnd 5: Ch 3, dc in each st around, join. Turn.

Rnd 6: Repeat rnd 4.

Rnd 7: Repeat rnd 3.

Rnd 8: Repeat rnd 4.

Rnd 9: Repeat rnd 3.

Rnd 10 - 11: Repeat rnd 4. Finish off.

Ave Maria Tree Skirt

Skill Level: Experienced
Materials:

- Size 10 Crochet Cotton Thread (see below for amounts)

  ○ Model made in red (MC), white (JC), green (CC)
- 0 / 3.25mm steel crochet hook
- Iridescent Seed beads (see below for amounts)
- Tapestry Needle to weave in ends

Gauge: One motif is 4.5" from point to point

Notes:
- This is a "Create your own" style of tree skirt. You determine how many rounds you need to make to reach the size you want. The border can be pulled out if years from now you need a larger skirt, making this truly an heirloom piece.
- The skirt is put together following the diagram at the end of the pattern. Once the beaded motifs are joined, small fill in motifs are added.
- Motif work is done with the wrong side and the beads will sit on the right side when finished.

  Amounts of thread needed per part of the skirt:
  - Motif: 16 yards and 99 beads
  - Motif border and join to one side: 2 yards
  - Motif border and join to two sides: 3 yards
  - Fill in motif: 3 yards
  - Final Border: 3 yards per number of motifs (4 total rounds of skirt took 113 yards).

Abbreviations and Special Stitches:
Double Crochet (dc)

Picot: Ch 3, sl st back into stitch

Beaded Chain (bch): Slide bead up to hook, ch 1

Beaded Single Crochet (bsc): Insert hook into stitch, pull up a loop, slide bead up to hook, yarn over and pull through both loops on hook.

Beaded Double Crochet (bdc): Yarn over, insert hook into stitch, pull up a loop, yarn over, pull through two loops on hook, slide bead up to hook, yarn over, and pull through both loops on hook.

The tree skirt is made of six wedges. The skirt is created by joining the motifs for each round before going to the next round. However, you can join this in which ever order you see fit. To determine how many motifs you'll need to make your skirt, you'll need to decide how many rows you want the skirt to be. If you need more rows than what is listed here, simply 12 motifs for each row (2 more for each wedge).

Number of Motifs needed for each round of the finished tree skirt: Round 1: 6 motifs Round 2: 18 motifs Round 3: 30 motifs Round 4: 42 motifs Round 5: 54 motifs

View of on e wedge of tree skirt

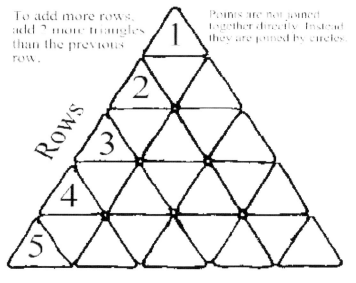

Layout of skirt

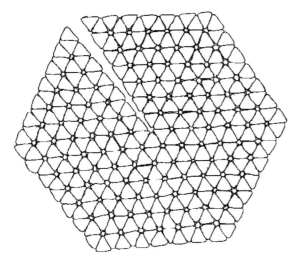

Instructions:

Motif:

Chain 4, join with sl st to form ring.

Round 1: Ch 2, bch, 2 bdc in ring, ch 3, (3 bdc, ch 3) twice; join with sl st to top of bch.

Round 2: Ch 2, bch, * bdc in each dc, bdc in space, ch 3, bdc in same space; Repeat from * around, join with sl st to top of bch.

Round 3: Ch 1, sc in same st, ch 4, skip 1 dc, ch 4, sc in ch sp, ch 4, sc in same ch sp, * (ch 4, skip next dc, sc in next dc, ch 4) twice, sc in ch sp, ch 4, sc in same ch sp; Repeat from * around and join with sl st in first sc.

Round 4: Sl st into space, ch 1, [(sc, bsc, sc) in next space, ch 1] twice, in next ch 4 sp work sc, hdc, bdc, ch 1, bdc, hdc, sc (corner made), ch 1, *[(sc, bsc, sc) in next sp, ch 1] three times, make corner; Repeat from * once more, (sc, bsc, sc) in space, ch 1, join with sl st into first sc.

Round 5: Sl st to next ch 1 sp, ch 1, bsc in same space, ch 5, bsc in next ch 1 space, ch 5, (bsc in ch 1 sp in corner, ch 5, sl st in same ch 1 sp) corner made, *(ch 5, bsc in next sp) 4 times, make corner; Repeat from * around, ch 5, join with sl st to first bsc.

Round 6: Sl st into space, ch 1, bsc in same space, ch 5, bsc in next space, ch 5 * bsc in corner space, ch 5, bsc in same space, ch 5, (bsc in next space, ch 5) 5 times; Repeat from * around ending with a sl st into first bsc.

Round 7: Sl st into space, ch 1, (bsc into space, ch 5) twice, * in corner work: sc, hdc, bdc, ch 3, bdc, hdc, sc, (ch 5, bsc into next space) 6 times, ch 5, repeat from * around and join with sl st to first bsc.

Round 8: Sl st into space, ch 1, sc into space, picot, ch 3, *sc into next space, picot, chain 3; Repeat around and join with sl st into sc.
Finish off and weave in ends.

<u>Joining motifs</u>:
To join the motifs, first a border is made of the motif and then the motif is joined to the next one. Most motifs are joined on one side only and then the last motif to finish the 'circle' is joined on two sides. See the diagram to follow the layout and the joining order.
Border: Join JC with a sl st to motif at a corner picot. * (Ch 5, sl st into next picot) 8 times, ch 5, sl st again in corner picot; Repeat from * around, joining with sl st to original sl st.
Lay the new motif (motif B) next to the motif it is to be joined to (motif A).

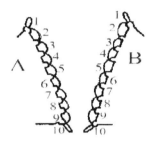

Join 1 side (see diagram): Sl st into B1 (this is the corner loop you just made in the border round), ch 5, sl st intoA1, ch 5, sl st into B2, ch 5, sl st intoA3, ch 5, sl st into B4, ch 5, sl st intoA5, ch 5, sl st into B6, ch 5, sl st into A7, ch 5, sl st into B8, ch 5, sl st into A9, ch 5, sl st into B10, ch 5, sl st into A10, ch 5, sl st into B9, ch 5, sl st into A8, ch 5, sl st into B7, ch 5, sl st into A6, ch 5, sl st into B5, ch 5, sl st into A4, ch 5, sl st into B3, ch 5, sl st into A2, ch 5, sl st into B1. Fasten off.

Join 2 sides (see diagram): Repeat as for 1 side but do not fasten off. At beginning corner, ch 5, sl st into next adjoining corner and repeat as for 1st side. Fasten off.

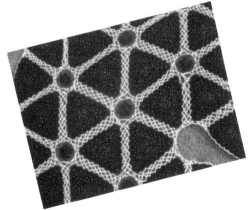

<u>Fill in motifs</u>: **Round 1**: With CC, ch 2. Work 12 dc in 2nd ch from hook, join with sl st. **Round 2**: Ch 2, dc in same st, 2dc in each st around, join with sl st. **Round 3**: Ch 3, sl st into corner loop from main motif, ch 3, sk 3 dc, sl st into next dc on fill in motif, * ch 3, sl st into next corner loop from main motif, ch 3, sk 3 dc, sl st into next dc on fill in motif; Repeat

<u>Final Border</u>:

With RS facing, attach JC with sc into a corner loop at the end of the opening side. * Ch 3, in next ch 5 loop work (sc, hdc, dc, picot, hdc, sc); Repeat from * around to last loop. Ch 3, in last ch 5 loop work (sc, hdc, dc, picot, hdc) and join with sl st to first sc. Fasten off.

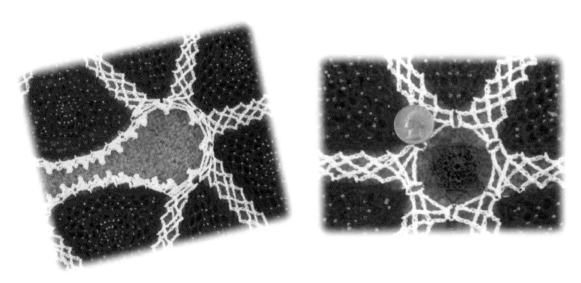

Musings from the Big Cheese...

As we were planning the CLF First Ever Book, talk of a second, third, and many other books began to rock our online message board. What next for the CLF? What more can we offer our members, and the crochet world at large?

I may be the "Big Cheese" and "Fearless Leader" of our group of wholesome minions, but I like input from the group before making decisions on what we'll have as projects and activities. It was decided that our Second Ever Book will be of a more "adult" nature...

Nothing Rated X mind you, rather some pretty trousseau items, flattering lingerie for those of us who've gotten a little wider and gravity (oh evil gravity) has affected, some fun "Hen Party" gifts, and maybe a little something sensual for the men folk as well...We'll see what the talented minds of the CLF come up with in the next few months...

For now, this final pattern should clue you in to the content in the next book! I fell in love with this design; it's sexy, sensual, and tasteful, just like the CLF!

Laurie Wheeler, August 10, 2008

Camano Island, WA

Peek-A-Boo Playtime Chemise

By Tracie McCorkle

This completely customizable pattern is a fun little number that can be worn as an outer garment if lined, or as-is for some, um, well, you know, "playtime." As you can see, this particular model wound up on a chandelier!

Before You Begin:

Measure yourself in the following areas:

- From the lowest curve of the breast to the center of the nipple—this will be known as measurement (N)
- The widest curve of same breast—this will be measurement (B)
- Around your chest area under the bust, as if measuring for a bra—this will be known as (C)
- At the bottom of the breast area to the hip (it's best to measure from the outside of the breast)—this will be (W)
- Around both hipbones, circling the waist—this is (H)

Special Stitches

3-dc cl: (3-dc cluster) (yo, insert hook into sp instructed, yo, pull through, yo, pull through 1st 2 loops on hook) 3 times, yo, pull through all loops on hook.

4-dc cl: (yo, insert hook into sp instructed, yo, pull through, yo, pull through 1st 2 loops on hook) 4 times, yo, pull through all loops on hook.

Materials:

Size 10 cotton crochet thread, or comparable thread of choice

¼" wide ribbon, 1-2 spools

US Size D crochet hook

Sewing needle w/ matching thread, optional

Stitch markers, optional

Directions:

Cups: (make 2) Make a foundation ch to the length of (N), adding 1-3 ch to make a multiple of 4, then add 3 more ch.

Row 1: Dc in 4th ch from hook, (dc, ch 2, dc) in same st, *sk 3 ch, (2 dc, ch 2, 2 dc) in next ch—dc shell made. Rep from * to end. In last ch work [(2 dc, ch 2) twice, 2 dc]—turning shell made. Continue in shell pattern on opposite side of foundation ch. Turn.

Row 2: [SI st to ch-2 sp of shell, ch 3, (dc, ch 2, 2 dc) in same sp]—beg shell made. Shell in ea shell, including turning shell, to end. Turn.

Row 3: Beg shell, shell in shell to top 4 shells at curved tip, (ch 1, shell in shell) 3 times, shell in shell to end. Turn.

Row 4: SI st to ch-2 sp, ch 4, (tr, ch 2, 2 tr) in same sp, (2 tr, ch 2, 2 tr) in next shell—tr shell made, dc shells to ch-1 sp, ch 1, shell in next shell, ch 1, shell in next shell, ch 1, shell in next shell to last 2 shells, work tr shells in last 2 shells. Turn.

Row 5: Beg shell, work shells in shells to shell before increase, ch 1, (shell in shell, ch 2) 3 times, shell in shell, ch 1, shell in shell to end. Turn.

Row 6: Work shells in shells to increase, ch 2, (shell in shell, ch 3) 3 times, shell in shell, ch 2, shell in shell to end. Turn.

Row 7: Work shell in shell until shell before increase, ch 1, shell in shell, ch 2, shell in shell, (ch 3) 3 times, ch 2, shell, ch 1, shell to end. Turn.

Row 8: Work shell to shell before increase, ch 1, shell, ch 2, shell, ch 3, (shell, ch 4) 3 times, shell, ch 3, shell, ch 2, shell, ch 1, shell to end. Turn. Continue adding increases of 1 ch between shells until cup is size desired. Finish off.

Assembly:

Placing cups next to each other with 2 bottom points overlapping to size, pin together. Attach crochet thread at outside end of cup and sc across, thereby working cups together. Measure the length of the cups across the bottom. Subtract this number from (C), and continue by making a chain to measure the rest of the length of (C) and adding 1-3 ch to make it a multiple of 4, join w/ sl st to 1st end of cups, being careful not to twist the ch. Do not finish off.

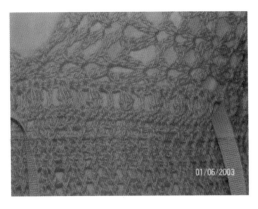

Band:

Rnd 1: Ch 1, sc in same st and in ea st around. Join w/ sl st to 1st sc. Ch 4, do not turn.

Rnd 2: *Sk next sc, work 4-dc cl in next st, sk next sc, ch 1, dc in next st. Rep from * around. Join w/ sl st to 3rd ch of ch-4. Ch 1, do not turn.

Rnd 3: Sc in ea st around. Join w/ sl st to 1st sc. Ch 3, turn.

Waist:

Rnd 1: Working in back loops only, dc in next 2 sc, *ch 1, dc in next 3 sc. Rep from * around, join w/ sl st in ch-3.

Rnd 2: Sl st to next dc, ch 3, fpdc in next st, *ch 1, sk ch-1 sp, fpdc in next dc, dc in next dc, fpdc in next dc. Rep from * around, ending w/ ch 1, fpdc, join w/ sl st to 1st dc. Ch 3, do not turn.

Rnd 3: Fpdc in next st, *ch 1, sk ch-1 sp, fpdc in next fpdc, dc in next dc, fpdc in next fpdc. Rep from * around, join w/ sl st to 1st dc. Ch 3, do not turn.

Rep Rnd 3 until Waist measures to (W).

Note: This ribbing pattern will cause the garment to curl outward, but will be corrected once properly blocked.

For the hip (H) measurements, add 2 increases per side every 3 rounds. Once (W) is reached, continue as follows:

Increase rounds:

Rnd 1: Continue as above, however increase in this round by working (fpdc in fpdc, 2dc in next dc, fpdc in next fpdc) 2 times per inch difference between the measurements of (W) and (H)—each increase step will work out to be ½" per finished increase. These increases should be placed randomly in this round, more practically in the sides of the garment.

If there is a large difference—more than 4", like me *blush*—work the increases at even intervals throughout the entire round instead of restricting them to the sides.

Rnd 2: Continue working as instructed above, except in each increase, work (fpdc in fpdc, 2dc in ea of the next 2 dc, fpdc in next fpdc).

Rnd 3: In ea increase, work (fpdc in fpdc, dc in next dc, fpdc in next 2 dc, dc in next dc, fpdc in next dc).

Rnd 4: In ea increase, work (fpdc in fpdc, dc in next dc, fpdc in next fpdc, ch 1, fpdc in next fpdc, dc in next dc, fpdc in next dc).

Rnd 5: Continue working round as in Waist. Repeat this round until length desired.

Edging:

Rnd 1: Sl st to ch-1 sp, ch 1, sc in same sp, *ch 5, sk next 3 dc, sc in next ch-1 sp. Rep from * around, end w/ ch 5, sl st into 1st sc.

Rnd 2: Sl st into ch-5 sp, ch 3, 2 dc in same sp while holding last loops on hook, yo and draw through all 3 loops, (ch 3, 3-dc cl) 4 times, *sk next ch-5 sp, (3-dc cl, ch 3) 4 times in next ch-5 sp, 3-dc cl in same sp. Rep from * around, join w/ sl st to top of ch-3.

Rnd 3: Sl st to 2nd ch-3 sp, ch 3, 2-dc cl in same sp, (ch 3, 3-dc cl) 2 times in same sp, ch 3, (3-dc cl, ch 3) twice in next ch-3 sp, 3-dc cl in same sp, sk next ch-3 sp, *between next 2 adjoining cls work (3-dc cl, ch 3) twice and 3-dc cl, sk next ch-3 sp, in next ch-3 sp work (3-dc cl, ch 3) 3 times, in next ch-3 sp work (3-dc cl, ch 3) twice, 3-dc cl in same sp, sk next ch-3 sp. Rep from * around, join w/ sl st to 1st 3-dc cl.

Rnd 4: Sl st to ch-3 sp, ch 3, 2-dc cl in same sp, *ch3, sk next cl, 3-dc cl in next ch-3 sp. Rep from * around, end w/ ch 3, join w/ sl st to 1st 3-dc cl. Finish off, weave in end.

Straps: (There will be 4 total, crossing the back to make an "X")

Join thread w/ sl st in one of the top two shells of either cup. *Ch 4, 2 dc in 3rd ch from hook. Rep from * to length desired, being certain not to twist strap, and long enough to reach to opposite side of back of garment (meaning, if strap is being worked from the right cup, the strap should be long enough to reach the left side of the back, placed below the left shoulder blade). Join strap at desired placement w/ a sl st. Finish off, weave in ends. Rep on same cup, joining thread in the next top shell. Rep these instructions for the opposite cup.

To finish:

Measure ribbon to 12-16" longer than (C). Weave through beading of the band area, making sure the clusters are on the outside of the ribbon. Tie in front with a bow. This ribbon may be sewn into place if desired.

If using 100% cotton thread, gently rinse in lukewarm water or hand-wash w/ mild soap. Gently squeeze out excess moisture, being careful not to wring the garment. Lay flat on a towel and roll up the towel, gently pressing on the towel as it is being rolled. Unroll the towel and gently tug the garment into shape. Lay

Just who is this "Fearless Leader",
"Big Cheese" person?

Name: Laurie Wheeler

Rank: Life long crocheter (at least 31 of her 39 years, she can't remember how old she was when she learned to hook!)

Yardage: Many, many thousands of yards. Laurie has crocheted her way across the world. From her home country of the USA, through college in England, throughout Europe, the Middle East, and Africa in her twenties, throughout a bad marriage, divorce, good marriage, and homeschooling two children, crochet has always played a role in her life and helped her maintain her sanity.

Laurie is a trained political analyst with a passion for crochet and yarn. She left her career in 1998 to raise her children and began an odyssey to figure out how to crochet clothing for them (without being able to read patterns); in 2001 she met Ann Hopkins who taught her how to spin her own yarn. This led to many an epiphany, including how under informed crocheters are about materials and their craft in general (that included her!). She began to design yarn specifically for crochet, and started to run into those folks she calls snobby pointy stick players (which doesn't include all knitters, just the snobby ones). Laurie was flabbergasted at the gall of some people who could be so rude about something so unimportant/yet important as a craft.

After several interesting discussions with fellow crocheters who had similar experiences and reading one too many threads on the Ravelry.com message boards that irritated her (and we can't forget having just watched "Monty Python's The Life of Brian" for the millionth time...) she started a group called The Crochet Liberation Front HQ on Ravelry.com.

Her mix of political and economic savvy, marketing experience, bizarre sense of the ridiculous, and deep dark desire to have crochet dominate the world has led to the members of the CLF to dub her, "Fearless Leader."

Laurie was perfectly content with "Big Cheese" and "Global Dominatrix" or "Budding megalomaniac", but since the minions entitled her Fearless Leader, she'll keep the title...